# VICTIM to VICTOR
## THE CHOICE IS YOURS

# The Road to Wholeness Series
## Healing of the Soul

# VICTIM to VICTOR
## THE CHOICE IS YOURS

BY Dr. RACHEL V JEFFRIES

A BOLD TRUTH Publication
Christian Literature & Artwork

# VICTIM to VICTOR

ISBN 10: 0-9991469-0-4
ISBN 13: 978-0-9991469-0-3

2ND *(EXPANDED)* EDITION

Rachel Jeffries International Ministries
P.O. Box 815
Hollister, MO 65673
www.rjim.org
*racheljeffries@msn.com*

Bold Truth Publishing
606 W. 41st, Ste. 4
Sand Springs, Oklahoma 74063
www.BoldTruthPublishing.com

06 17 ▪ 09 17                              10 9 8 7 6 5 4 3 2

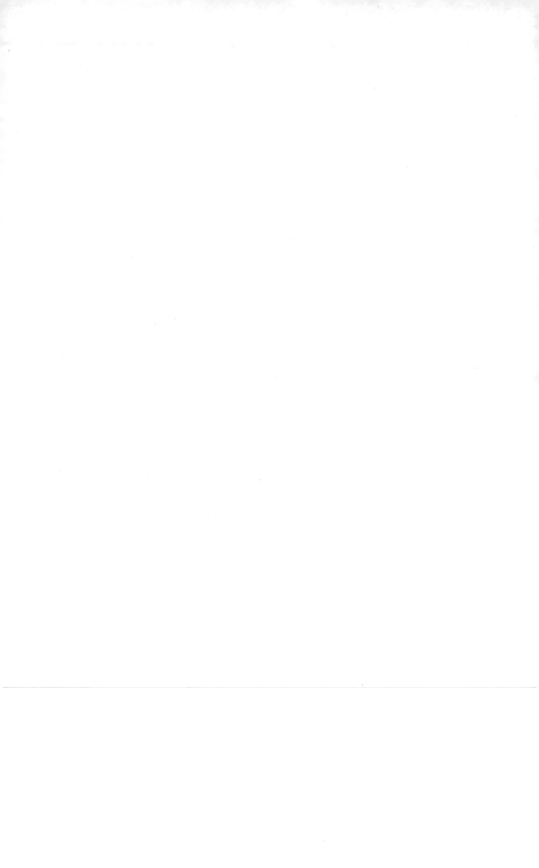

# Contents

# Contents

# Preface

When I became familiar with the victim mentality or the victor mentality, it was new to me.  It was like a bell rang in my heart.  It was such a release to know that we could guard ourselves in this area of always being victimized, and come forth with such victory.

When we have had, bad things happen over and over, it is easy to get into the victim mentality.  This kind of thinking will mar our ability to move forward. It can and will paralyze us in our ability to have vision.  For all we can see on every side are causality, death and destruction. Some people have everything in life but still have this mentality of the world owes me.

*Proverbs 29:18 says where there is no vision the people perish: but he that keepeth the law happy is he.*  The first part of this Scripture shows us what happens when we lose our vision.  We start the death process.  We may not die physically but we lost our way in life, in the soul and spirit.  To keep this victim mentality out of our lives is very important.  Satan uses this mentality to stop us from doing our very best in life. It can also be the root cause of illness.

If you have lived a life of abuse, you will more than likely have to deal with this victim thinking.  One of the things we will cover in these lessons and study will be recognizing abuse and overcoming it.

There is such a victim mentality in our world today.  We need to acquaint ourselves with the both mentalities so we can see

# Preface

the true way of thinking.   When we watch the news, we see the world fighting for the victim's chair.  Unfortunately, we see this same spirit in the home, church and workplace.

The purpose of this study is to help us to be healed in our soul.

God does have a plan, purpose and intention for our life.

We have prayed the Holy Spirit will open the doors to the hearts of those who need this study.  For you to have these materials is a direct answer to prayer.  I believe God has guided you to it.  We pray you can receive all God has for you in your study of these materials.

No matter who you are or what you have become, you may have experienced being victimized at least once in your Christian life.

The purpose of this study is to help you walk through any difficulty in the past, present or future.  God has given hope for your future.

# Topics

*Jeremiah 29:11*
*For I know the thoughts and plans that I have for you,*
*says the Lord, thoughts and plans for welfare and not*
*for evil to give you hope in your final outcome.*

*1 Corinthians 15:57*
*Thanks be to God, which giveth us the victory through*
*our Lord Jesus Christ.*

Subjects covered in this study:

What is a victim mentality?
- Recognizing this thought pattern
- What is my vision of myself? (Victim or Victor)

How do I overcome this victim thinking?
- Training my mind to think differently
- Accepting God's word on the matter
- Deliverance of Fear

What is abuse?
- Physical
- Sexual
- Verbal
- Emotional
- Spiritual

What is an enabler?
- The difference between forgiveness and enabling
- Forgiveness vs. unforgiveness

# Topics

Are you a user or a giver?
- Accepting the nature of Jesus Christ

What is a rescuer?
- Recognizing rescuing actions

Letting God heal me of Victim Thinking
- *Psalms 4:7*
- *Psalms 13:5*
- *Psalms 15:2*
- *Proverbs 4:21-24*
- *Luke 6:45*
- *Ephesians 6:6*

Renewing my Mind
- Filling my Mind with God's Word
- Doing the Word of God
- Thinking Like my inheritance in Christ

These are the topics included in this Road to Wholeness, Emotional Healing Lessons.

We have asked the Holy Spirit to come and open our understanding that we may be made free from the victim mentality and switch to the victor thinking in every area. I pray you are encouraged in your life after completing these studies.

Other subjects available in this Road to Wholeness Series are:
- Pitiful or Powerful, *The Choice is Yours now published* and available on www.rjim.org or www.amazon.com

# Topics

In reading the Table of Contents and Outline of this study, do you see any areas you are seeking God for knowledge?

Do you have questions concerning abuse?  If so, write them down.

_____

_____

_____

_____

When you have completed this study, look back in your notes and see if the Holy Spirit has answered them for you.

_____

_____

_____

_____

Have you ever thought you might be enabling someone to abuse you or enabling them to abuse someone else?

_____

_____

_____

_____

Do you see yourself as a victim?  If so, what area?

_____

_____

_____

_____

# Topics

Write down how the victim thoughts and mentality can be overcome.

_____

_____

_____

_____

Has God enlightened you in how to minister to the abused? If He has, write down usable material revealed to you by the Holy Spirit.

_____

_____

_____

_____

_____

**Notes:** _____

_____

_____

_____

_____

_____

_____

_____

_____

_____

_____

_____

# CHAPTER 1
## Choosing Victim or Victor

∎

At some time in our lives many of us have felt victimized and have not walked like a victor in life or in relationships with others. There may be things that have happened in your life that you don't understand now. Sometimes you may experience various feelings which make it difficult to cope; such as fear, anger, sorrow, etc. In these classes we will define how our thinking can be changed as we discover the nature of God, the nature of the enemy, and our own nature with and without Christ.

**We can become victims or victors in our thinking** and change the lives of our children and ourselves. It is a **choice** we make each day in every situation we face. We have been trained either to be a victim or victor.

*Deuteronomy 29:29* tells us,
*The secret things belong to the Lord our God: but those things which are revealed belong unto us and to our children for ever, that we may do all the words of this law.*

# VICTIM to VICTOR

*Deuteronomy 30:19*
*I call heaven and earth this day against you, that I have*
*set before you life and death, blessing and cursing: there-*
*fore choose life that both thou and thy seed may live.*

Sometimes we have made bad choices in friendships, places we visited, and things we have done. It is not what happens to us that makes us a victim; but our thinking concerning that incident. If I blame someone else for my being a victim, I will stay in victim thinking. If you make a mistake, do not get into self-condemnation, but learn from it. If it is sin, then ask forgiveness from the Lord.

*1 John 1:9 NIV*
*If we confess our sins, he is faithful and just and will for-*
*give us our sins and purify us from all unrighteousness.*

In my life, I have had many opportunities to be a victim. Once someone took everything I had worked for, for over a year. I felt helpless, powerless, and despondent. It took time for me to work through those feelings. I had lots of regrets for allowing it to happen. I felt I had to go over the things in my mind constantly. I did not want it to ever happen to me again. God showed me things in the natural and the supernatural to guide me past what had happened. I started by **forgiving** the person, and then giving them what they had taken. My flesh did not want to do that. My family wanted me to stand up and fight back. A trusted minister was in our home as a guest, and I told them the story in my pain. The pain of loss was taking me down. At that point I had to move forward or death would take me. I was losing ground emotionally and spiritually. They told me, *"You know what to do."*

I answered with a question, *"What?"* You must give all they took verbally and release it. I got on my knees and cried bitter tears of release. My flesh did not want to give to them what they had taken. But in obedience I did it. I can say when I got up from that prayer, I could sense a new freedom taking place inside me.

I had every right to go to court and stop their actions. I had chosen not to. Since that time, I have learned I must take and keep my spiritual authority always. Satan is the one who comes out against us and our fight is not with flesh and blood. Despite that season of time, God opened doors for me worldwide. Even though the enemy meant it for evil, God turned it for my good. It was during the episode someone was there and heard me speak. God then used them to open a much larger door to the nations for me. Nothing the enemy tries to destroy us with can succeed.

There are times we may need to go to court to stop enabling people from harming us. Many times people are law-suit happy. They become defiant, and ready to fight. Revenge is victim and vindictive thinking, it is never successful.

There could be a time you must have a law suit. At other times, the Holy Spirit may say, **"the battle is mine, not yours."** Either way, it is God who wins the battle for us as we turn it completely over to Him. The Holy Spirit will strengthen us with revelation knowledge that transforms our thinking through the Word.

> *Romans 12:1-2*
> *1 I beseech you therefore, brethren, by the mercies of God, that ye present your bodies a living sacrifice, holy, acceptable unto God, which is your reasonable service. 2 And be not conformed to this world, but be ye transformed by the renewing of your mind, that ye may prove what is that good, and acceptable, and perfect, will of God.*

To be transformed means to change, transfigure, transform. It comes from another Greek word meaning to fashion, to form the idea of adjustment. (Strong's Concordance -3445). Webster's dictionary states, to change the nature, the condition or function of. It means to convert, to turn, to change from one form or use to another.

The Word of God changes and transforms us when we read and study the Scriptures. Our natural man does not like the discomfort of change and wants everything to stay settled, just the way we like it.

The Bible speaks of change in 2 Corinthians.

> *2 Corinthians 3:18*
> *But we all, with open face beholding as in a glass the glory of the Lord, are <u>changed</u> in to the same image from glory to glory, even as by the Spirit of the Lord.*

*2 Corinthians 5:17*
*Therefore if any man be in Christ, he is a new creature: old things are passed away; behold, all things <u>are become new.</u>*

*John 3:7*
*Marvel not that I said unto thee, Ye must be <u>born again</u>.*

When we are born-again, things are fresh and new. **<u>We are changed.</u>** Our mindset needs to be: *"I am going to grow, no matter what the demands of change may bring in my life."*

Some reasons why I **do not like change** are:

1._____

_____

2._____

_____

3. _____

_____

If I were to **change something** in my life, what would it be? Write it down. It has been proven that those who write down goals will accomplish more.

_____

_____

_____

_____

_____

_____

If I am asking for change in my life, then I need to ask God what my part is. Some things involve other people and their wills and those we cannot change. We must give them over to God, and let His power change the situation.

## Liking Change Too Much

If I like change too much, this can cause instability. This kind of thinking can keep us from being rooted and grounded in the Lord. We can run from preacher to preacher, from church to church, to friend to friend and never grasp what God has for us. If someone did you wrong in one church, the same thing is likely to happen in the next.

I know someone right now who is being abused in a church and the Holy Spirit is keeping them there. There may be times He will hold you steady during a bad situation. He may have a purpose you cannot understand. We must listen to our spirit to hear what God would have us do.

**Notes:** _____

_____

_____

_____

_____

# CHAPTER 2
## Defining Victim, Victor, and Victimization

■ ■

*The word <u>victim</u> means to separate, something being killed, destroyed, injured, or otherwise harmed by or suffering from some act, condition or circumstance. Such as victims of a disaster. It also means a person who suffers loss by being swindled.*

*<u>Victim</u> also means one who suffers injury, loss, or death because of a voluntary undertaking. One tricked, swindled, or taken advantage of.*

*<u>Victim Mentality</u> is a capacity, endowment, inclination or an outlook that causes you to think you are harmed or suffering from some act.*

*<u>To victimize</u> means to subject to harm or danger. It also means to dupe, cheat, fraud or swindle.*

Many times the Holy Spirit warns us inwardly not to connect to certain people or things and we go ahead and move in that direction anyway. Sometimes we miss the signals because we feel we are thinking badly about another person, when in reality it is the Holy Spirit warning us; this is not the right connection.

Victim mentality is the thought, we are always being wronged by someone or some circumstance and are never responsible for our actions. We do not realize this kind of thinking is easy to fall into.

We can become victims of our own thinking and develop self destructive or self sabotaging behavior. We must train ourselves to listen to our spirit. God gives us inward warnings. It reduces the chances of being at the wrong place at the wrong time. Knowing our authority in Christ and speaking the power of the Blood of Jesus over us simply keeps us safe. Having faith in the power of that Blood keeps us from these bad things happening all the time. Confession from our mouth of *Psalms 91* is so vital always. It is our security. We do not just think it but we say it. "He has given His Angels charge over me to guard me and protect me in all my ways." We cannot blame God when we did not listen. Forgive yourself and purpose to follow God's impressions closely. Paul's writings in the Epistles are where the Church is to live today. We have authority over principalities and powers. An example is a lady who felt a warning not to go to the bank now. She overrode the feeling and the bank was robbed while she was there. She had quoted *Psalms 91* before she left home but overrode the warning. She was puzzled on what happened. She was speaking to a minister of the Word of God about why it happened.  He wondered as well.  Then the Holy Spirit prompted him to ask her if she got an inner check in her spirit about not going at that time.  She said, yes, she did but thought it was just her own thoughts.  So, we need to pay attention to these inner checks and warnings.

## PLACING BLAME ALWAYS ON SOMEONE ELSE OR CIRCUMSTANCES

Another example is a person who is always late for church, work, or anywhere they go.  You can hear coming out of their mouth, *"It was my wife, husband, or children who made me late."*  Instead of saying, we stayed up last night until midnight and watched movies: we did not wake up on time today.  *"I am not to blame, the person got in my way, so I hit them."* or *"I was born poor and I guess I will just have to stay that way."*  Sometimes when rudeness is practiced, the excuse is, I was never taught manners in my home, so this is just the way I am.  Excusing all of our actions as someone else's fault is very unhealthy emotionally. We need to ask God for healthy relationships.

We do get warnings as guidance from the Lord. Sometimes I moved in a direction I thought was right, but hit a hard spot.  When that happens, I get before God and ask Him if He wants me to move this way or is the enemy trying to stop me from getting what God has for me?  I have seen people miss going to a conference they needed to attend because things started happening to stop them.

I have missed an accident by seconds when I turned on a wrong road and it slowed me down. I made a turn which I almost never make. That wrong turn possibly saved my life, or at least saved me from a horrible accident. When my friend and I arrived in the area close to our home, we saw a vehicle air-borne cross in front of us. If we had just been moments earlier, we would have been in an accident. It happened the vehicle had come loose from the truck pulling it and veered into our lane. God always watches out for us and saves us from being a victim more times than we know.

## Victimized in Finances

If it is victimizing in the area of finances, we may have opened the door through fear of poverty and want. You may be spending emotionally by thinking you must buy things as others do. As we apply the Word of God that instructs us to tithe and give to others, God will rebuke the devourer for our sakes. Scriptures that follow will help you.

*Malachi 3:10-11*
*10 Bring ye all the tithe unto the storehouse, that there may be meat in mine house, and prove me now here- with, saith the Lord of hosts, if I will not open you the windows of heaven, and pour you out a blessing, that there shall not be room enough to receive it.*
*11 And I will rebuke the devourer for your sakes, and he shall not destroy the fruits of your ground . . .*

*Joel 2:25*
*And I will restore to you the years that the locust hath eaten, the cankerworm, and the caterpillar, and the palmerworm, my great army which I sent among you.*

Sometimes we have to do things in the natural to stop the onslaught against our finances. We may have to open new bank accounts and make sure that we use our credit cards with discretion. Our finances can be stolen by identity theft as others have used our credit cards illegally. I have had my bill payments stolen out of the drop-off mailing box in front of the post office. Someone hooked a box on a wire and pulled up the mail during the night and my bills were some that were stolen. When I kept getting requests for my bills to be paid, I contacted the bank, the person that I owed, the post office and the police. Not only did the person take my check, but he stole my time also. Now I take precautions by praying over every piece of mail I send. If it is a bill, I pay extra postage to have them sign they received it. Taking responsibility can prevent you from being a victim. Pleading the blood of Jesus over things as we mail them is a great protection. But listening to the Holy Spirit about taking out insurance, receipt of letter requested, or other things He may prompt us to do to protect ourselves is important as well.

If we are always blaming someone else for things which happen to us, we are **victim thinkers**. We must recognize our part in any failure happening to us. For example: If every place I **work**, I am let go of the job within a short time, then I probably need to ask myself what is wrong. I may have a spirit of denial which is keeping me from seeing the main reason I fail over and over. Examine your heart about being a team player and not a lone ranger. Ask yourself, are you adaptable to do things the way they want you to? You can blame yourself so badly that you cannot move forward. Then the enemy will pour on condemnation to victimize you again. With the Holy Spirit's help make the adjustment and move on.

Many times when a person has been **divorced**, they put all the blame on the other party. They should look into their own thinking and ask if they did anything to contribute to the problem. When we recognize our mistakes, and learn from them we are better off as a person. I do realize in these cases there are people who make up their mind they do not want to be married anymore as they cannot or will not face responsibility. In such a case, we have no blame or shame.

List some things that you are blaming others for.

1. _____
2. _____
3. _____

Write down what you could have done to change the situation.

1. _____
   _____
2. _____
   _____
3. _____

Ask yourself, have I forgiven the person involved in this incident? If I am still unforgiving in my heart toward them, I become their victim by giving them my time, my energy, and my peace. I have the responsibility to release them to God and be free from it.

> *"Forgiveness is unlocking the door to set someone free and realizing you were the prisoner."*
> - Unknown

## Are you a Victimizer?

If you are the one who is doing the victimizing, usually you try to make another person feel guilty for your own actions. It goes something like this: *"If you had not been there at that time, I would not have done that to you."* If it is sexual abuse, the victimizer tries to make you keep it a secret. They do not want anyone to know and may threaten harm if you tell anyone. Or say that they will commit suicide if you tell. They put the blame on the victim instead of themselves. If we are someone's victim we usually do not see it coming. How to recognize victimization: If someone is pushing me to do something that I do not feel right about, I need to stand up and be bold. We may innocently walk into situations. There are all kinds of scams these days. There are new ones every day. Keep yourself filled with knowledge and listen to your inner man. Inner checks will come and we must pay attention.

**Three signs that someone may be trying to victimize me are:**
- 1. Pressing me to do something that I do not feel is right.
- 2. Manipulating me by using flattering words to take advantage of me.
- 3. Lavishing gifts upon me to assure them of favors later.

We cannot be whole with this kind of thinking. If we are the victimizer, we need to come to terms with it and get help. If we are the abused victim, we need to tell someone trustworthy, pray for strength, and overcome the fear by using the Words of Paul in

*Romans 8:37*
*"Nay, in all these things, we are more than conquerors through Him who loved us."*

or

*Philippians 4:13*
*"I can do all things through Christ which strengthened me."*

**Notes:** _____

_____

_____

_____

_____

_____

_____

# CHAPTER 3
## Faith or Fear, Which Will It Be

■ ■ ■

*Faith believes for good things to happen.*

*Fear believes for bad things to happen.*

It is hard to overcome the behavior of victimizing because those doing the harm do not recognize their behavior as being abusive. The world offers little hope for those for abusers. Usually an abuser has been abused in his own life, and as such learned the behavior. Once he is aware of his wrongdoing, it is easier for him to change. The Holy Spirit will deliver and set him free. He will change his heart, to be gentle and loving, if he will allow Him to.

*Galatians 5:1* says I am to *stand fast in the liberty where with Christ hath made me free and not be entangled again with the yoke of bondage.*

Paul is speaking of the believers' liberty being taken through legalism. He was trying to get them to think more of the heart being circumcised by Christ rather than the outward man. Circumcision was a cutting away of the flesh for the purpose of cleansing; it is the same in the Spirit. We are to cut away the fleshly desires in order to be clean before God and man.

In the Amplified Bible *Galatians 5:19-21* says these *works of the flesh are immorality, impurity, indecency, idolatry, sorcery, enmity, strife, jealously, anger, (ill temper), selfishness, divisions, (dissensions), party spirit (factions, sects, with peculiar opinions, heresies), envy, drunkenness, carousing, and the like. I warn you beforehand, just as I did previously, that those who do such things will not inherit the kingdom of God.*

The works of the flesh open the door in our life for the enemy to step in and take over our very soul. The demon spirits walk into our lives, through the works of the flesh by using our very own spirit. In order to overcome these works of the flesh, we must meditate on God's Word.

*Philippians 4:8* tells us *whatsoever things are true, honest, just, pure, lovely, and things that are of a good report, virtuous, and praiseworthy, we are to think upon these things.*

I heard of an incident where a young man filled his eyes with sinful things by watching a movie with some friends. They were not bothered by the scenes on the screen, but it made the young man feel unclean. His father asked him what he did to overcome this situation. He said, *"When I got home, I read my Bible for a long time. The more I read, the more at peace I became."* The Bible speaks of this as being a cleansing power from the Word of God.

> *John 15:3*
> *"Now ye are clean through the Word which I have spoken to you."*

In this instance do not keep on going back and watching the kind of thing that troubled your soul. Find a new avenue to put your energy into.

**Notes:** _____

_____

_____

_____

_____

_____

_____

_____

_____

_____

_____

_____

_____

_____

_____

_____

_____

_____

_____

# VICTIM to VICTOR

**Notes:** _____

_____

_____

_____

_____

_____

_____

_____

_____

_____

_____

_____

_____

_____

_____

_____

_____

_____

_____

_____

_____

_____

_____

_____

_____

_____

_____

# CHAPTER 4
## Developing a New Image

■ ■ ■ ■

### HOW DO YOU SEE YOURSELF?

In *Habakkuk 2:2*
> *And the Lord answered me, and said, Write the vision, and make it plain upon tables, that he may run that readeth it.*

Do you have a vision for your future life? What would you like to do? Write it down. A vision is a goal with a deadline.

_____

_____

_____

_____

_____

Do I believe in my heart that through Christ I can complete this vision?

_____

How do I see myself?  Write some attributes that define who you are inside.  Do not write your vocation.  Examples: kind, loving, caring, or friendly.

1._____    4._____
2._____    5._____
3._____    6._____

Then, some negative aspects of yourself and how you act at times. Examples: procrastinate, lazy, bossy, jealous, proud, depressed or sad.

1._____    2._____
3._____    4._____

If you find there are more negative things, then write what your plan is to overcome them.  Make a plan of action to overcome them.

_____
_____
_____
_____

## WHAT ARE YOU SAYING ABOUT YOURSELF?

Another form of identification is what others hear you say about yourself. Do you often talk in the negative saying, *"I am sick'* or *"I am coming down with a cold!"* When you constantly say things like this, your thinking has become distorted and creates victim mentality.  To replace this kind of thinking, write down and say often, *"I am healed."*

> *Psalms 107:20*
> *He sent His word and healed them, and delivered them from their destructions.*

## Write some positive things about who you are in Christ.

Let us think about things we are because of <u>our relationship with Christ.</u>  Search your heart for who the Word says you are. Write those words of who you are in Christ then find a Scripture in the Bible that backs these words up.

1. **I am righteous:** *...that we might be made the righteousness of God in him. - 2 Cor. 5:21b*

2. **I'm satisfied:** *...for He satisfieth the longing soul. - Ps. 107:9*

3. _____

_____

_____

4. _____

_____

_____

5. _____

_____

_____

6. _____

_____

_____

Gideon is an example of someone who saw himself through the identity of his family. His family was poor and he was the least in his father's house. He did not see himself as God did: "a mighty man of valor." But God did! In *Judges 6:1-13* we are told Gideon did not have confidence in what God was telling him. He could only see himself as a victim of his circumstances. Gideon made some negative confessions about himself. He could only see what was in front of him—the weakness and his lot in life.

Chapter 6 of Judges, he saw himself as a victim. **All of life's circumstances held him in bondage in his thinking.**

## A list of Gideon's circumstances:

► (1) God had delivered his people into bondage because of their evil deeds.

► (2) The Midianites were prevailing over Israel.

► (3) The people of God were hiding in the mountains, and caves.

► (4) The enemy was destroying their crops, sheep, and donkeys.

► (5) They were outnumbered by the enemy.

► (6) Their enemy came in to destroy.

► (7) Israel was impoverished.

► (8) His father worshipped idols.

What God saw about the situation:
- ▶ (1) The children of Israel cried in prayer to him.
- ▶ (2) The Lord sent a prophet.
- ▶ (3) God reminded them of their past times of deliverance.
- ▶ (4) God sent an angel.

When Gideon caught on to God's vision for him, his thinking began to change. He realized he could not win the battle alone and looked to God for help. There is a difference between humility thinking and victim thinking.

In *verse 12*, the angel of the Lord said unto him he was a mighty man of valour. The first question Gideon asked the angel of the Lord, if the Lord is with us, why then is all this befallen us? Have you ever asked that question? Have you ever asked the Lord why?

If it is sickness, perhaps we have done something to harm our body. Some people can get into feeling so much remorse they cannot function. God does not want that. The secret is not to allow condemnation to surround you. Feelings may say if the Lord is with me, why is this happening? But the renewing of our minds by the power of the Word can take us to know beyond a shadow of a doubt that the Lord is with us.

The following Scriptures can be taken as medicine. (Read every day out loud and meditate upon them until you see a change).

*Job 9:27b*
*I will leave off my heaviness and comfort myself.*

*Isaiah 61:1-3*
*1 "The Spirit of the Lord is upon me; because the Lord hath anointed me to preach good tidings unto the meek; he hath sent me to bind up the brokenhearted,*
*2 to proclaim liberty to the captives, and the opening of the prison to them that are bound; to comfort all that mourn;*
*3 "To appoint unto them that mourn in Zion, to give unto them beauty for ashes, the oil of joy for mourning, the garment of praise for the spirit of heaviness; that they might be called trees of righteousness, the planting of the Lord, that he might be glorified."*

*Isaiah 61:7*
*For your shame ye shall have double and for confusion they shall rejoice in their portion: therefore, in their land they shall possess the double; everlasting joy shall be unto them.*

*Proverbs 12:25*
*Heaviness in the heart of man maketh it stoop: but a good word maketh it glad.*

*Hebrews 13:5*
*Let your conversation be without covetousness; and be content with such things as ye have for he hath said, I will never leave thee, nor forsake thee.*

*Hebrews 13:5 AMP*
*Let your character or moral disposition be free from love*

*of money [including greed, avarice, lust, and craving for earthly possessions] and be satisfied with your present [circumstances and with what you have]: for [God] Himself has said, I will not in any way fail you nor give you up nor leave you without support [I will] not, [I will] not in any degree leave you helpless nor forsake nor let [you] down (relax My hold on you) [Assuredly not!]*

*Joshua 1:5*
*"There shall not any man be able to stand before thee all the days of thy life: as I was with Moses, so I will be with thee: I will not fail thee, nor forsake thee."*

I hear people say, we should meditate on the Word of God. The problem is our western mindset is not always familiar with meditation. **The word *meditate* means to reflect upon, study or ponder, to think deeply and continuously.**

You will be able to think upon the things of God in the midst of lots of people. You can develop such a consciousness of God's holy presence that you are listening to Him while hearing other people, too. When I travel, and am in a room full of people speaking another language, inside I am communicating with God at the same time they are talking. You too, can have such an awareness of His presence and the Word.

Most of us can relate to Gideon. When pressure comes, we choose to think on the things that are true, honest and of good report.

**Gideon means warrior. It means to destroy anything, to cut asunder, down or hew down.**

God knew Gideon had the power to cut the enemy asunder. Gideon had forgotten who he was through the circumstances of life. In Bible times, names meant something. Each person was named according to the plan of God for them. Of course, not everyone fulfilled what their name meant. The choice was theirs. Maybe God has given you a glimpse of what He has planned for you, and you cannot see yourself that way. The Lord kept working with Gideon one thing at a time. Each time he obeyed God, he got closer to what God had in mind for him. If God gave us the whole plan of our lives at once, it would make us afraid, or we would be overwhelmed in our thoughts and not be able to function.

God called Gideon, a mighty man of valor. Did this change his victim mentality? It took time but it eventually did. God has time for us. He can change our thinking if we allow Him to.

God has said of you and me in *2 Corinthians 5:17* we are new creatures in Christ. *Therefore, if any man be in Christ, he is a new creature: old things are passed away; behold all things are become new.*

Did you notice it says here things become new? When we come into Christ, we are a new creature now. The old things have passed away now. ***Behold all things are become new.***

**Become means to come to be, to grow to be; change or de-**

**velop into by growth.** The illustration used in the dictionary is about a tadpole becoming a frog. Another is the caterpillar becoming a butterfly or a moth. The ability to become either one of these things is the process going on inside it. Through growth all things become new. Through growth we become mature. When we give our lives to Jesus, we start a new life immediately. This new life develops, changes and grows into a mature person into one like the Lord Jesus Christ.

Gideon did not see any way the problem with the Midianites could ever be solved. The Midianites were destructive and were ruining everything Israel was trying to accomplish. This is exactly what Satan tries to do to us. He comes in to destroy everything we are trying to do for God. Thank God, Jesus has won the victory over him. We do not have to hide. We must use our authority over the enemy. We are made overcomers by the Word of our testimony and the blood of the Lamb.

You may have come to Christ having been in prison, prostitution, and you have allowed shame to enter into your heart. The devil will whisper, *"There is no way out of this mess!"* He wants to keep you enslaved. I heard from a friend of mine who visited prisons. Everyday the guards would constantly tell the inmates, *"When you get out, you will be right back here in no time."* They would drill it in their heads everyday. Faith comes by hearing, we must know the process of faith building words for a person to say *"No, I won't be back in here."* Cut off the power of those evil words over your life. Choose not to believe those words. Forgive the ones who spoke those word curses over you. You cut them off by saying out loud *"I curse the power of those words against me." "I render them powerless against me in the name of Jesus."*

The **Midianites** fighting against Israel were descendants of Abraham. Their name means **contentious or brawling.** They should have been like Abraham, but they were not. They gave Israel many bad times. Their choice was to always fight.

The following Scripture backs up they were descendants from Abraham.

According to Genesis, the Midianites were the descendants of Midian, who was a son of **Abraham** through his wife Keturah: *"... again Abraham took a wife, and her name was Keturah. And she bare him Zimran, and Jokshan, and Medan, and Midian, and Ishbak, and Shuah" (Genesis 25:1–2, King James Version).*

**Notice that God refers to fighting as being valor, warrior, and mighty. But the nature of the fight on the enemy's side is being contentious. Satan only counterfeits God's Kingdom.**

In *John 10:10* we see the nature of God and the nature of Satan. The nature of Satan is to steal, kill, and destroy. The nature of God and Christ is to give life more abundantly.

> *John 10:11* says,
> *I am the good shepherd: the good shepherd giveth his life for the sheep.*

This verse shows us the nature of the shepherd that it is good and not evil. When we come into emotional, physical, and spiritual healing, it is of utmost importance to know the nature of Christ.

> *John 10:12-14*
> *12 But he that is a hireling, and not the shepherd, whose own the sheep are not, seeth the wolf coming, and scattered the sheep.*
> *13 The hireling fleeth, because he is an hireling, and careth not for the sheep.*
> *14 I am the good shepherd, and know my sheep, and am known of mine.*

In these verses, we see clearly both natures, the nature of Jesus and the nature of Satan. If we do not remember our authority and take back territory that which Satan has stolen from us, we will continue as victims until we die.

**We must choose to see ourselves as a victor and not a victim.** In the victim thinking we can get to a place seeking after other people's mercy. Then we can become addicted to that mercy.

There are people no matter how much God does for them, they do not see it. They want the strokes from other people. They seek merciful people out just to tell their tale of woe. We must restrain ourselves if we have been in that pattern. We must retrain our way of thinking and acting. We can only do that through the help of the Holy Spirit and through the power of the Word of God.

# VICTIM to VICTOR

**A person who is delivered from a victim mentality does something about his circumstances.** He does not sit still and wait for something to happen to change it all. He acts with the Word of God and gets delivered.

> *Psalms 34:6, 10*
> *6 This poor man cried, and the Lord heard him, and saved him out of all his troubles.*
>
> *10 The young lions do lack, and suffer hunger: but they that seek the Lord shall not want any good thing.*
>
> *Psalms 31:4*
> *Pull me out of the net that they have laid privily for me: for thou art my strength.*

[Privily means to hide (by covering over) lay privily, in secret.]

In this verse when David felt hemmed in he said, "*Pull me out of the net that they have laid privily for me: for thou art my strength.*" When David told God how he felt, he began to speak of who God was to him and how he trusted Him. David did not stay hemmed in.

In *verse 7*, God had considered his trouble. He said, **I will be glad and rejoice in thy mercy: for thou hast considered my trouble. Thou hast known my soul in adversities.**

In *verse 8*, he spoke God had set his feet in a large room. Again, we see that he knew the nature of God. Man had hemmed him in, but God had made his feet to be in a big room.

In reading *verses 9-13 of Psalms 31* he cried, **Have mercy upon me, O Lord, for I am in trouble: mine eye is consumed with grief, yea, my soul and my belly. For my life is spent with grief and my years with sighing: my strength faileth because of mine iniquity, and my bones are consumed. I was a reproach among all mine enemies, but especially among my neighbors and a fear to mine acquaintance: they that did see me without fled from me. I am forgotten as a dead man out of mind: I am like a broken vessel. For I have heard the slander of many: fear was on every side: while they took counsel together against me, they devised to take away my life.**

If you or I have ever felt like *verses 9-13* we just cannot stop there. In *verse 14* David said, *But I trusted in thee, O Lord: I said Thou art my God.* Never stop until you confess God's greatness into an issue or problem.

I suggest that you take time to write down the things dealing with trouble and grief in any area of your life which may have caused you to feel like David.

_____

_____

_____

_____

_____

In *Psalms 31:19-20* he began to say, **O how great is thy goodness, which thou hast laid up for them that fear thee: which thou hast wrought for them that trust in thee before the sons of men! Thou shalt hide them in the secret of thy presence** *from the pride of man: thou shalt keep them secretly in a pavilion from the strife of tongues.*

What a promise we have when we are in trouble.  I have asked the Lord to hide me at times and He has.  What do you believe that **God's nature** is concerning those problems you wrote in the above?

_____

_____

_____

_____

When we look back at *Judges 6:9,*  we see **Gideon** had forgotten what God had said to him. *I delivered you out of the hand of the Egyptians, and out of the hand of all that oppressed you, and drove them out from before you, and gave you their land.*

When pressure is on, it easy to forget the words spoken concerning those challenges we are facing.  In this Scripture, He tells us the children of Israel did evil in the sight of the Lord, and He delivered them into the hand of the Midianites for seven years.  Even in their disobedience God made a way of deliverance through Gideon.

**Notes:** _____

_____

_____

_____

_____

# CHAPTER 5
## Availing Ourselves of Our Advocate

■ ■ ■ ■ ■

Thank God for Jesus. He has delivered us. In the New Testament, we are free in Christ. If we have sinned, we have an Advocate with the Father.

> *1 John 2:1*
> *My little children, these things write I unto you, that ye sin not. And if any man sin, we have an advocate with the Father, Jesus Christ the righteous.*

The word **advocate**, in the Strong's Concordance means, *an intercessor, consoler, or comforter.*

**The Webster's New College Dictionary** says **advocate** means *one who supports or defends a cause and one who pleads in another's behalf.*

> *1 John 1:6-9 states,*
> *6 If we say we have fellowship with him and, walk in*

*darkness, we lie, and do not the truth;*
*7 But if we walk in the light, as he is in the light, we have fellowship one with another, and the blood of Jesus Christ cleanseth us from all sin.*
*8 If we say we have no sin, we deceive ourselves and the truth is not in us.*
*9 If we confess our sins, he is faithful and just to forgive us our sins, and to cleanse us from all unrighteousness.*

Who has defeated the enemy for us? Think about what He has done for you. Write down some things God has done to help you in the past and or present.

_____
_____
_____
_____
_____
_____
_____
_____
_____

*1 John 2:12* says,
*I write unto you, little children, because your sins are forgiven you for his name's sake.*

So, I would ask, *"Are we laboring over sins that have been forgiven?"*

*Psalms 23* speaks about our soul being restored. Sin does mar our souls; but **God is in the restoration business.** Our soul is our mind, will and emotions.

## Victorious Thinking

We have studied the meaning of victim and taken time to work with it. We need now to meditate upon what a victor is. It means one that vanquishes, or defeats an adversary or an opponent. We have the victory over the adversary, the devil. Some of our souls have been exposed to things that have opened the door to him; but we can shut those doors. We can be healed and set free from the victim mentality and go forward into the victor mentality. I can say *"Yes, those things happened to me, but Jesus defeated the enemy."* Therefore, I can walk in victory in Him because He purchased my freedom.

In the movie **"The Gladiator"** we see men putting helmets on with shields in front of them. The guys who knelt held the shields in front. The ones, who were standing, held their shields to hold a box over them. They protected each other. We have such shields in the Holy Spirit.

*Isaiah 54:17* is one of those shields. It says that *no weapon formed against me shall proper.* It also says I will prove them to be in the wrong.

**Since He said it, and He is God Who cannot lie, then it must be so!**

*Hebrews 6:18 states*
*That by two immutable things, in which it was impos-*
*sible for God to lie, we might have a strong consolation,*
*who have fled for refuge to lay hold upon the hope set*
*before me.*

*Numbers 23:19*
*God is not a man, that he should lie; neither the son*
*of man, that he should repent: hath He said, and shall*
*He not do it? Or hath He spoken, and shall He not do*
*it? Or hath He spoken, and shall He not make it good?*

When sickness came to me, I had to keep sending it back to
its source. I had to keep the Scriptures before me that He
was not a God that would lie.

## Some healing Scriptures are listed below from the Word of God.

*Job 33:25*
*Then man's flesh shall be restored; it becomes fresher*
*and more tender than a child's and he returns to the*
*days of his youth.*

*3 John 1:2*
*Beloved, I wish above all things that thou mayest pros-*
*per and be in health, even as thy soul prospereth.*

*Hebrews 12:12-13*
*12 Wherefore lift up the hands which hang down, and*

the feeble knees;
13 and make straight paths for your feet, but that
which is lame be turned out of the way; but let is rather
be healed.

*Philippines 2:13*
For it is God which worketh in you both to will and to
do of His good pleasure.

*Romans 8:22*
He that spared not His own Son, but delivered Him up
for us all, how shall He not with Him also freely give
us all things.

*Deuteronomy 7:15*
And the Lord will take away from thee all sickness, and
will permit none of the evil diseases of Egypt which
thou knowest, upon thee.

*Jeremiah 30:17*
For I will restore health unto thee, and I will heal thee
of thy wounds, saith the Lord...

**Notes:** _____

_____

_____

_____

_____

_____

**Notes:** _____

_____

_____

_____

_____

_____

_____

_____

_____

_____

_____

_____

_____

_____

_____

_____

_____

_____

_____

_____

_____

_____

_____

_____

_____

_____

_____

_____

_____

# CHAPTER 6
## Training Our Minds

■ ■ ■ ■ ■ ■

Becoming a victim in most instances is not something that we walk into on purpose, but walking as a victor is something that we must do on purpose. **We must train ourselves to have the Victor mentality.**

### How do I train my mind to think differently?

*Romans 8:6-7 says,*
*6 For to be carnally minded is death; but to be spiritually minded is life and peace.*
*7 Because the carnal mind is enmity against God: for it is not subject to the law of God, neither indeed can be.*

To be **carnally minded** means relating to sensual desires and appetites. Earthly, temporal, and always thinking of what we desire in the flesh. The carnal mind will fight against the spirit. Our spirit is hungry for the Word of God. Our fleshly mind tells us we never need to read the Word. Our mind wants to do what is fun or feels good. Sin in some cases may feel good, but the rewards are evil. Life is a continual battle of the wills until our mind is renewed and our life transformed.

Brother Kenneth E. Hagin teaches how he overcame the **victim mentality** of always being sick and depressed. He did what he could do. If he was weak or could hardly move, he would attempt to move what he could. He would read *Mark 11:23-24* about moving mountains by believing in your heart. He did not lie in bed and complain about how bad it was. He heard people all around him telling him it was God's will for him to suffer. He had to begin to **confess what God was saying** rather than what religious people thought. Our thinking has to be changed by what we see in God's Word. We must pay attention to who and what we are exposing ourselves to.

**We have a choice** every day to either see ourselves as being defeated or see ourselves as a victor. We must choose to get into a vein of thinking what agrees with God's Word. So often what we see is the opposite of God's will and desire for us. We can change things by **saying** what God says and then experience His rewards.

> *Hebrews 11:6b* states,
> *...for He who comes to God must believe that He is, and that He is a rewarder of those who diligently seek Him.*

That is awesome! <u>Believing God is the rewarder</u> must come to the forefront of our thinking.

**Religion** has caused wrong thinking about the nature of God. It may suggest you take a vow of poverty when God says, *I will supply all your needs.* This is victim thinking by choice. It is rebellion against God's Word for us to think this. Some may believe they are pleasing God, but they have bought into religious thinking instead. Some of the religions that advocate such thinking have large temples worth millions of dollars. If pleasing God is to be broke, then why do they build such large buildings lavished with ornate decorations? I am not against the costly buildings or the ornate decor, but if we are to be poor, why have a few chosen to be rich? The rest of us will be victims of poverty, to which I say, *"No thanks, I do not think so."* We must not be deceived into thinking religiously. If God meant for us to be poor, then who is going to feed the poor? We need to think like God and not like religions and the world.

The Word states in *Romans 10:17, So faith cometh by hearing and hearing by the Word of God.*

The same verse in the Amplified Bible says, *So faith comes by hearing [what is told] and what is heard comes by the preaching [of the message that came from the lips] of Christ (The Messiah Himself).*

If we say with our mouths, we are healed by the stripes of Jesus and the next minute confess we are going to die; we will not be healed. This is called wavering and double mindedness.

*James 1:7-8 says,*
*7 That man should not expect to receive anything from the*

*Lord.*
*8 He is a double minded man, unstable in all his ways.*

The negative confession cancels out the faith words.

In Kathryn Khulman's meetings miracles would happen for people who did not believe. They would be healed through the working of miracles.

> *1 Corinthians 12:27-31 NKJV*
> *27 Now you are the body of Christ, and members individually.*
> *28 And God has appointed these in the church: first apostles, second prophets, third teachers, after that miracles, then gifts of healings, helps, administrations, varieties of tongues.*
> *29 Are all apostles? Are all prophets? Are all teachers? Are all workers of miracles?*
> *30 Do all have gifts of healings? Do all speak with tongues? Do all interpret?*
> *31 But earnestly desire the best gifts. And yet I show you a more excellent way.*

The above Scriptures show there are various workings in the Body of Christ. Some operate strongly in miracles. I attended Ms. Kathryn Khulman's meetings and it was evident she operated in the gift of miracles. I heard testimony after testimony of those who came and they were scornful and skeptical of her. She allowed God to work among the people. The people would be drawn by the Spirit of God to come to the stage. There would be there many who did not believe but were healed. Many did not know Christ until the moment they were healed. That was truly a gift from God. She allowed worship to take place. The worship and the people getting their eyes on the Lord caused many profound miracles.

I was in one of her meetings with a back issue. I rode on a tour bus with a group going to her meeting. I was miserable while riding. An anointing came over my back like a heat wave and my back was instantly healed. No one touched me, no one called me forward, and nothing was said about healing of backs was taking place. It was supernatural. To this day, I have not been in the pain I was in the day I attended the meeting.

I believe most kept their healings. This is where learning the Word of God and putting it into our life, helps us stay healed. We do not have to wait for a miracle service. We can have the anointing anytime through the power of God's Word. I have noticed others who operate in this gift of healing or miracles. Benny Hinn is an example. He sat under Ms. Khulman's ministry many years. He watched and listened. The same anointing drew him. Billy Burke operates in a miracle anointing and numerous people are healed. God wants us well and He has provided many ways for us to receive our healing.

When I was twelve years old, I was attacked with appendicitis. It was while I was playing the piano for our church. I had a horrible pain in my side. They rushed me to the hospital and my dad carried me in. It was on a Sunday night. In our small town, there were two doctors. This one was the one our family trusted.  We drove six miles to his hospital where he came in just for me.  He diagnosed and said, *"I would like to keep her overnight and do surgery tomorrow morning."* My dad was protective in some ways.  He told the doctor my daughter is too young to be cut so we are going to take her home.  But the church had been praying.  A little while after I left the hospital all the pain left.  That was the church's prayers for me being answered.  I still have my appendix.

Then there is the laying on of hands and anointing with oil for healing.

> *James 5:13-15 New Life Version*
> *13 Is anyone among you suffering? He should pray. Is anyone happy? He should sing songs of thanks to God.*
> *14 Is anyone among you sick? He should send for the church leaders and they should pray for him. They should pour oil on him in the name of the Lord.*
> *15 The prayer given in faith will heal the sick man, and the Lord will raise him up. If he has sinned, he will be forgiven.*

In the book of Acts they anointed aprons and placed them on people's bodies and they were healed.  Today we call them prayer cloths.  The pastor or those delegated to do so, anoint the cloths with oil and they are given to those who have requested them. Some are distributed to those who are unable to attend.

> *Acts 19:11-12*
> *11 And God wrought special miracles by the hands of*

*Paul:*
*12 So that from his body were brought unto the sick handkerchiefs or aprons, and the diseases departed from them, and the evil spirits went out of them.*

My Mother believed strongly in the power in prayer. She would ask for prayer cloths and place them in my unsaved Dad's pillow. If any of us needed healing she had anointing prayer cloths pinned to our clothing. It may sound crazy to some, but it is scriptural and it works. My dad came to know Jesus. When Mother passed on to Heaven, every pillow in the house had prayer cloths pinned to them.

Have you ever noticed those who say, "Healing is not for to-day," They don't see healings like those who believe? If the person who leads the ministry says, *"There will never be a healing line in my church or ministry,"* they do not have healings in their ministry.

Years ago, the Pastor of the Lutheran Church we were part of during the Charismatic revival laid hands on a lady who came from Russia. She had requested to have hands laid on her and anoint her with oil for healing of cancer. Even though it had never happened in the church, the Pastor read *James 5:13-15* to the congregation and showed them it was scriptural. The lady was completely healed.

There are numerous ways God has provided for us to receive our healing. Healing is for today!

**Notes:** _____

_____

_____

_____

_____

_____

_____

_____

_____

_____

_____

_____

_____

_____

_____

_____

_____

_____

_____

_____

_____

_____

_____

_____

_____

_____

_____

_____

# CHAPTER 7
## Recognizing Double Mindedness
■ ■ ■ ■ ■ ■ ■

In *1 Corinthians 12:10* speaks of the working of miracles as a gift of the Holy Spirit. Those of us who are in the house of God and have the power of the Word in our lives must learn to discipline our minds. The mind fluctuates. One minute it thinks: *"Wow, I am healed!"* The next minute it can think, *"I will never be healed."*

*James 1:8* calls this being **double minded** or having a double soul. In the ***Strong's Concordance,*** it says, **two spirited, vacillating (in opinion on purpose).** It comes from a root word meaning twice minded. Also, it means to waver in opinion, doubt.

James 1:7-8 the Amplified Bible says, *for truly, let not such a person imagine that he will receive anything [he asks for] from the Lord, [For being as he is] a man of two minds (hesitating, dubious, irresolute), [he is] unstable and unreliable and uncertain about everything [he thinks, feels, decides].* Being double minded can cheat us out of the blessings the Lord desires to bring into our lives. The only thing that can keep us from being double minded is believing and accepting God's Word on any matter.

Our prosperity begins by knowing what God desires for us.

> *3 John 2 says,*
> *I wish above all things that thou mayest prosper and*
> *be in health even as thy soul prospereth.*

*Psalms 34:1-9* tells us what to focus on and say, *I will bless the Lord at all times: His praise shall continually be in my mouth. My soul shall make her boast in the Lord: the humble shall hear thereof, and be glad. O magnify the Lord with me, and let us exalt his name together. I sought the Lord, and he heard me, and delivered me from all my fears. They looked unto him, and were lightened: and their faces were not ashamed. . . O fear the Lord, ye his saints: for there is no want to them that fear him.*

To fear the Lord means to reverence the Lord. To revere also means to respect with profound awe and devotion. (**Webster's New Collegiate Dictionary**) To worship God would be a definite meaning here. We respect God in daily life, not just when we are in church.

We respect what it says in *2 Corinthians 5:17. If any man be in Christ, he is a new creature: old things are passed away, behold all things have become new.* We have respect for the

Truth in God's Word and can believe it and stand on it all our lives.

*Proverbs 8:13* states, *The fear of the Lord is to hate evil ...* So, if we reverence God we will hate evil. We will not walk as close to evil as we can and hope that we will not get burned. No, we will obey the Word.

One of the things that can draw us into becoming a victim is fear of man. We need deliverance from this type of fear.

> *Proverbs 29:25*
> *The fear of man brings a snare.*
>
> *Hebrews 13:6*
> *So that we may boldly say, The Lord is my helper, and I will not fear what man shall do unto me.*

With terrorist activity being a possibility these days, we must stay on top of the spirit of fear. When the threats come and plans are made to attack us, the best way to live is to keep the Word of God active in our lives. We must live in the following Word from the Lord:

> *Ephesians 6:10-15, 18*
> *10 Finally, my brethren, be strong in the Lord, and in the power of his might.*
> *11 Put on the whole armour of God, that ye may be able to stand against the wiles of the devil.*
> *12 For we wrestle not against flesh and blood, but*

*against principalities, against powers, against the rul-*
*ers of the darkness of this world, against spiritual wick-*
*edness in high places.*
*13 Wherefore take unto you <u>the whole armour of God</u>,*
*that ye may be able to withstand in the evil day, and*
*having done all, to stand.*
*14 Stand therefore, having your loins girt about <u>with</u>*
*<u>truth</u>, and having the breastplate of righteousness;*
*15 And your feet shod with the preparation of the <u>gos-</u>*
*<u>pel of peace</u>.*

*18 <u>Praying always</u> with all prayer and supplication in*
*the Spirit, and watching thereunto with all persever-*
*ance and supplication for all saints.*

Negative words are powerful against us. The only way to overcome them is to speak the truth in God's Word which is more
powerful. We must not respect something else above God's
Word. The respect should always be for what God has said. This
is the way to keep anxiety away from our hearts. The Word says
that in the last days men's hearts will fail them because of fear.
We are living in that time now, so stay fixed in the Word of God.

*Luke 21:25-26*
*25 And there shall be signs in the sun, and in the moon,*
*and in the stars; and upon the earth distress of nations,*
*with perplexity; the sea and the waves roaring:*
*26 Men's hearts failing them for fear, and for looking*
*after those things which are coming on the earth: for*
*the powers of heaven shall be shaken.*

We cannot overcome fear by ourselves. We say and agree with *2 Timothy 1:7* which says, *"For God hath not given us the spirit of fear; but of power, and of love, and of a sound mind."* God's Word has authority. To **magnify** means *to exceed.* When we look through a magnifying glass, things become larger. The Word is like that. It becomes larger than the problem. The Word of God concerning any issue makes the problem small.

As we studied earlier about **double mindedness,** I would like to go over that again. If we say with our mouths one minute that we are healed by the stripes of Jesus, and the next minute we say we might die from a sickness; we are **double minded.** Our mind lines up with the Word of God at first and then the next minute it does not. To be consistent by speaking the truth in God's Word brings victory.

## Being of a Carnal Mind

To be **carnally minded** is something easy for the human being. We must train ourselves to think in line with God's Word.

To be **carnally minded** means *relating to sensual desires and appetites. Earthy: temporal, to always be thinking of what we desire in the flesh* is to be carnally minded.

<u>The New World Dictionary</u> says in or of the flesh; bodily; material or worldly, not spiritual.

*Romans 8:6-7*
*6 For to be carnally minded is death; but to be spiritu-*

*ally minded is life and peace.*
*7 Because the carnal mind is enmity against God: for it*
*is not subject to the law of God, neither indeed can be.*

*James 1:7-8*
*7 For let not that man think that he shall receive any*
*thing of the Lord.*
*8 A double minded man is unstable in all his ways.*

In the Strong's Concordance it means two spirited, vacillating (in opinion on purpose). It comes from a root word meaning twice minded. To waver in opinion, doubt.

## SOULISH HEALING

Our prosperity starts in our souls. That is why we need healing in our souls. **The three parts of the soul are:** **the mind, the will, and emotions.** Physical healing begins in the souls of men. When we get to the root cause of illness or poverty, we find the soul has a big part to play.

**The three parts of our being are:** **spirit, soul and body.** God wants us whole in every area. We are a spirit, living in a body with a soul.

*1 Thessalonians 5:23*
*Now may the God of peace Himself sanctify you completely; and may your whole spirit, soul, and body be preserved blameless at the coming of our Lord Jesus Christ.*

*3 John 2*
*Beloved, I wish above all things that thou mayest prosper and be in health, even as thy soul prospereth.*

The Amplified translation says, *Beloved, I pray that you may prosper in every way and [that your body] may keep well, even as [I know] your soul keeps well and prospers.*

*Proverbs 3:5-8*
*5 Trust in the Lord with all thine heart; and lean not unto thine own understanding.*
*6 In all thy ways acknowledge Him, and He shall direct thy paths,*
*7 Be not wise in thine own eyes: fear the LORD, and depart from evil.*
*8 It shall be health to thy navel, and marrow to thy bones.*

Worry is in the mind which is the soul area. We are a three part being. Spirit, soul and body. Often the soul is thought of as the part which goes to heaven. **The soul has three parts, the mind, the will and the emotions.** God desires to do things for us but if we are unwilling, He will not violate our wills.

Depression is in the soul area. Dr. Don Colbert says, *"Ten percent of people have chemical imbalances. It is impossible to be depressed without "Stinking thinking." "Most of our behavior is learned and can therefore be unlearned even if it's rooted in one's genes."*

Part of our soul is our emotions. Dr. Colbert quote: *"Emotions do not die. We bury them but we are burying something that is still alive."* Emotions buried alive never die.

An example he uses is one twenty-five-year-old woman's husband confessed he desired to leave her to pursue a male companionship. She developed numerous ailments to keep him close to care for her during her bad days, which bad days became every day.

Often folks are in the prayer line for healing but their mind is not set to become well. I am not the judge and neither are you but I know I have seen it numerous times. Either the welfare check or disability would stop and the fear of the unknown takes hold of them.

One time a man told me, *"God keeps me sick so I can go around the country telling people about Jesus and I am being paid."* His mind was made up. I tried to talk to him and show him Scriptures but he wanted no part of it. He did not care what the Word of God said, he wanted it his way. It was self-deception. I wondered what kind of Jesus he was telling folks about.

I have heard others say, *"I have been prayed for by and they name the healing evangelist and if God wanted me well, then I should've been well by now."* They have gone from healing service to healing service but never believing God wants them well. God will not violate our will.

I believe in being touched by the anointing through healing

evangelists, but Jesus is the Healer. Our eyes must stay on Him.

Let's review *3 John 2*. The Amplified translation says, *Beloved, I pray that you may prosper in every way and [that your body] may keep well, even as [I know] your soul keeps well and prospers.*

The Word of God has the final say so on this. Every mental challenge can be healed. Many have allowed their mind to become demonically influenced. It is important what we place before our eyes and our ears. Choices are before us to have life or death, God has said in His word, and I paraphrase, God's suggestion is "Choose life."

> *Deuteronomy 30:19*
> *I call heaven and earth as witnesses today against you, that I have set before you life and death, blessing and cursing; therefore choose life, that both you and your descendants may live.*

**Notes:** _____

_____

_____

_____

_____

_____

_____

_____

_____

_____

**Notes:** _____

_____

_____

_____

_____

_____

_____

_____

_____

_____

_____

_____

_____

_____

_____

_____

_____

_____

_____

_____

_____

_____

_____

_____

_____

_____

# CHAPTER 8
## Recognizing Types of Abuse
■ ■ ■ ■ ■ ■ ■ ■

<u>There are various kinds of abuse:</u> **physical, sexual, verbal, emotional or mental, and spiritual abuse.** There are times we do not realize what abuse is. We hear about so much abuse these days. The following is an example:

One day I was driving around slower than I would normally when a man in a car behind me got very angry. He had plenty of room to pass me but he chose to ride my bumper. I looked in my rearview mirror and saw that he was very angry. He was shaking his fist and yelling something which I chose not to listen to. He finally drove up beside me and yelled at me. I was quoting the Word of God and just let him rage on. That made him angrier. I am sure he could not hear me, but I was quoting my widow Scriptures from *Proverbs 15:25* saying, *"the border of the widow is established."* Later in this teaching I will give you the meaning of established. However, we will deal with the word **border** right now. In Strong's Concordance #1366 in the Hebrew border means *boundary, the* *territory enclosed, limit, quarter, space.* The widow has many promises in which God encloses them and places boundaries around them. We must learn to call on the Word of God in all situations. The Scripture says no man can curse that which God has blessed. I chose to bless the angry driver with better sense and kept on going without fear. He finally passed me. Fear could have gripped me as it is situations like that which make folks get out of their car and hurt someone. However, I believe keeping myself in faith and not in fear, just made him go away.

I was saying you cannot curse that which God has blessed. This question arises in *Numbers 23:8 How shall I curse, whom God hath not cursed? Or how shall I defy whom the Lord hath not defied?*

A causeless curse cannot even light on me. *Proverbs 26:2* says, *As the bird by wandering, as the swallow by flying, so the curse causeless shall not come.*

This man certainly showed the attributes of being an **abuser**. On this occasion the Word was magnified. The Word was bigger than this fellow's anger and it sure brought comfort to my heart. If you had asked this man if he were an **abuser** I am sure he would have said he was not. An abuser, most of the time, does not see themselves the way they are.

## SEXUAL ABUSE

One of the most damaging types of abuse is <u>**sexual abuse**</u>.

We see such a case mentioned in the Bible within David's family.

*2 Samuel 13:1-20* in the *Amplified* says,
*1 Absalom Son of David had a fair sister whose name was Tamar, and Amnon [her half brother] son of David loved her.*
*2 And Amnon was so troubled that he fell sick for his [half] sister Tamar, for she was a virgin, and Amnon thought it impossible for him to do anything to her.*
*3 But Amnon had a friend whose name was Jonadab son of Shimeah, David's brother; and Jonadab was a very crafty man.*
*4 He said to Amnon, why are, the king's son, so lean and weak-looking from day to day? Will you not tell me? And Amnon said to him, I love Tamar, my [half] brother Absalom's sister.*
*5 Jonadab said to him, Go to bed and pretend you are sick; and when your father David comes to see you, say to him, Let your sister Tamar come and give me food and prepare it in my sight, that I may see it and eat it from her hand.*
*6 So Amnon lay down and pretended to be sick: and when the king came to see him, Amnon said to the king, I pray you, let my sister Tamar come and make me a couple of cakes in my sight, that I may eat from her hand.*
*7 Then David sent home and told Tamar, Go now to your brother Amnon's house, and dress him meat.*
*8 So Tamar went to her brother Amnon's house, and he was in bed. And she took dough, and kneaded it, and*

*made cakes in his sight, and baked them.*

*9 And she took the pan and emptied it out before him, but he refused to eat. And Amnon said, Send everyone out from me. So, everyone went out from him.*

*10 Then Amnon said unto Tamar, Bring the food here into the bedroom so that I may eat from your hand. So Tamar took the cakes which she had made, and brought them into the room to Amnon her brother.*

*11 And when she had brought them unto him to eat, he took hold of her, and said unto her, Come lie with me, my sister.*

*12 She replied, No, my brother! Do not force and humble me, for no such thing should be done in Israel! Do not do this foolhardy, scandalous thing!*

*13 And I, how could I rid myself of my shame? And you, you will be [considered] one of the stupid fools in Israel. Now therefore, I pray you speak to the king; for he will not withhold me from you.*

*14 But he would not listen to her and lay with her.*

*15 Then Amnon hated her exceedingly; so that his hatred for her was greater than the love with which he had loved her. And Amnon said to her, Get up and get out!*

*16 But she said, No! This great evil of sending me away is worse than what you did to me. But he would not listen to her.*

*17 He called the servant who served him and said, put this woman out of my presence now, and bolt the door after her!*

*18 Now [Tamar] was wearing a long robe with sleeves and of various colors, for in such robes were the king's virgin daughters clad of old. Then Amnon's servant brought her out and bolted the door after her.*

*19 And [she] put ashes on her head and tore the long, sleeved robe which she wore, and she laid her hand on her head and went away shrieking and wailing.*

*20 And Absalom her brother said to her, Has your brother Amnon been with you? Be quiet now, my sister, He is your brother; take not this matter to heart. So Tamar dwelt in her brother Absalom's house a desolate woman.*

**Whoa! What a sad thing!!** Tamar had nothing to do with this situation, yet she had to dwell in her brother's house as a desolate woman. This episode caused a lot of problems in David's family. There was much abuse in this situation. We see her father did not discern the situation and did not protect her. **Her brother had all the wrong friends. He got advice in all the wrong places.** He was deceitful and totally dishonest. He caught her off guard and destroyed her reputation. What happened to her affected the whole family. Absalom covered his brother's sin and kept a deadly secret. He acted like nothing serious had happened to Tamar. He was asking her to keep this quiet by telling her not to take this to heart. He minimized what happened to her physically, mentally and emotionally by ignoring her despair. Satan works in darkness and in secret. There is much we can learn from this story.

**One of the first red flags** - Why did he want her alone to himself? Why does he watch her prepare food? Why did he bolt the door so no one else was to come in? **After the horrible thing happened, she was told by her brother Absalom to be quiet.** The **shame** of this happening was the reason they wanted it kept quiet. This is one reason **sexual abuse** is so prevalent in today's society. The woman is put to shame while the abuser makes the victim look like the guilty party. Many women hold inside of them the anger, the hurt, and the shame of what happened to them. Young men being abused by other men is the same issue. Their abuser makes them feel like no one would ever believe them, so it must be kept a secret.

I heard of an incident where a young woman was **sexually abused** by her brothers from an early age. They would bring their friends over and they would use her too. Their family moved often and everywhere they moved, her brothers molested her and brought various young men to do the same. She said after 100 young men used her, she lost count and felt it would never come to an end. She became a prostitute while a teenager. **The redemptive power of God touched her life.** Today she has a lovely family and she is a precious person. She is healed in spirit, soul, and body. The power of the Holy Spirit is marvelous. She and another young woman are prayer partners. God answers their prayers so wonderfully. The delivering power of God is the only thing which can heal souls in this kind of situation.

## VERBAL ABUSE

The other form of **abuse** is <u>verbal abuse.</u> Unfortunately, this is a common form of abuse. The abuse in this Scripture of Tamar was sexual and verbal. **Abuse** means *to de-file, to overdo, and to mock.* *Her brother was more afraid of repercussions than taking care of the situation.* When reading about this horrible happening my heart hurts for her. A brother should never abuse his sister, ever!

## SPIRITUAL ABUSE

*Galatians 2:4*
*And that because of false brethren unawares brought in, who came in privily to spy out our liberty which we have in Christ Jesus, that they might bring us into bondage.*

Since the word **abuse** *means misuse*, we know all abuse is the same. We do not expect <u>spiritual abuse</u>. There have been those in the church who have misused people financially. We need the Holy Spirit gift of discernment.

Recently in the news there was story of a married youth pastor who brought many young men into bondage through the sexual things he did to them.

<u>Perversion</u> is certainly of the devil. It is his nature to pervert everything he can. Some of us remember the **Jim Jones** incident. He was a spiritual cult leader who poisoned several hundred people because he was caught in abuse by one of our senators or congressman. He did not want the truth to come out so he killed hundreds of his followers; forcing them to drink poison Kool-Aid.

A pastor is to be a shepherd - not a sheep herder. **Sheep do not drive very well** and should never be whipped. We all need correction, but it should be done in love.

Years ago, we had an experience with sheep of our own. The two sheep knew our voice, when it was time to be fed, they would come running. One day we were going to load them in an enclosed trailer to take them to a neighbor's barn, but no one could get them into the vehicle. They tried driving them with the dog (a border collie trained to round up sheep), but they would not do anything for the dog. I kept saying, *"If you will just get some food and place it in your hands, they will follow you anywhere."* Since I was new at dealing with sheep, no one listened to me. Finally, I went to the barn and got some food and came up close to the sheep. Sure enough, they followed me right into the trailer. They knew me and trusted me. When you feed sheep the correct food every day, they will grow to trust you and will follow you. You must never drive them to do what is needed. Simply feed them, lead them and they will follow you; sheep are natural followers. You might say they are dumb, but no they are not. If you get to know them you will find they are very smart. One day my sheep saw me sitting on the porch step praying with tears in my eyes. She came up on the porch on the top step behind me. With her lips she began to wipe my tears. Then with her mouth played with my hair. It was an adorable moment. Someone said to me when I told them about this experience, *"Sheep don't do things like that."* Of course, I could say, *"Mine does."* I knew her and she knew me.

Get to know the sheep. When something hurt our sheep like a thorn caught in their mouth or their wool, they would come and baaa until we noticed and could help them.

## SELF ABUSE

In *1 Samuel 31:4* Saul said unto his armour-bearer, *Draw your sword and thrust me through, lest these uncircumcised come and thrust me through and abuse and mock me. But his Armour-bearer would not, for he was terrified. So Saul took his sword and fell upon it.*

One form of **abuse** in this Scripture is <u>**self abuse**</u>. Saul was going to fall on his own sword. He even asked someone to kill him. We can abuse anything. Usually we think of abuse as coming from someone else outside of us. It is not always that way. Saul abused himself. We often hear of young people, who are cutters. Something has caused them pain in their life and they add pain to pain. They need deliverance in their soul. Jesus heals souls! He delights in it.

Another example of **self-abuse** is when a person constantly berates themselves. I have heard people say, *"I am dumb, everything I do is wrong, all I ever have is bad luck. My family said, "I would never amount to anything. I guess they were right."* This goes on and on without realizing they are into self-abuse. Their words drive nails into a coffin which ruins their success. It sets a pattern of mental anguish. It is a learned behavior and thinking pattern. To change it like any other form of abuse it must be recognized for what it is and overcome it. Some call these word curses, I call it self-abuse. It really hurts the listeners who love the person to hear these words. Ultimately, they are abusing the hearers as well. To break this pattern, you start saying the opposite. Don't just think it but verbalize *"I am smart, witty, everything I do is a success. I have a bright future. I am a new creation in Christ."*

*Ephesians 4:29* says, *"Let no corrupt talk come out of your mouths, but only such as is good for building up, as fits the occasion, that it may give grace to those who hear."*

I highly recommend a book about this subject written by a young woman I know well. The book is on www. amazon. com titled **LIES THE DEVIL TOLD ME!** *by Emma Byers.*

## MISUSE OF PEOPLE AND BLESSINGS

In the **New Collegiate Webster Dictionary** the word **abuse,** means *to use wrongly or improperly; misuse.*

Misusing our things is another form of abuse. Some of us are abusing our bodies through over-eating, drugs, and alcohol. We could be misusing things God has given us for His glory. If He has blessed us with a home, a car, furniture, or business, these should be kept clean and in order.

# CHAPTER 9
## Recognizing Abuser Personality Traits
■ ■ ■ ■ ■ ■ ■ ■ ■

As we look at the **soul of the abuser** we find certain **personality traits**. An abuser comes with angry actions, strong body language, lies and accusations. Usually they are manipulative and controlling. When I say controlling, I mean misuse of their authority or taking authority that does not belong to them. All of us have some area of control or authority. We either have responsibility for something or someone. We all answer to someone outside of ourselves. The abuser answers to no one. If they get into a position where they must answer to someone, they usually refuse to come face to face with what they are doing wrong. The abuser tries to blame someone else for their actions. It is not uncommon for them to place the blame on the person they are abusing. They make that person feel that they have caused it. Everyone around them has to walk on eggshells as they blow little things out of proportion. <u>Example</u>: You could not remember to turn the lights off as you are leaving the room. A normal person would remind you to turn them off. They may even help you by turning them off for you and talk to you later. The **abusive person** rants, screams, throws things, shouts, embarrasses, and sometimes even hurts someone else physically over such a small thing. They are always upset and angry inside.

On the other hand, the abuser can be sweet in many ways. They are like an alcoholic which seems to have two souls. **One is sweet, loving, and caring while the other is angry, forceful and mean.** Their actions affect everyone around them. They usually feel very remorseful even a few minutes later and will even cry in some cases. Maybe they just took a gun and held it in your face, but they have remorse immediately. They will apologize and beg for your forgiveness. Soon after, they act like they did not do anything. Their excuse is, you said something they did not like which is the reason they acted that way. They usually promise to never do it again. They use your reaction as a way of manipulation or control. **They are addicted to fear** and expect you to be afraid. In some cases they love to see your tears. They may even comfort you over what they did to you. They want you to be dependent upon them as your only source of comfort.

*Keeping secrets is another trait of the abuser.* They count on your not telling anyone else what they are doing to you. They may even threaten to kill you if you tell anyone else. Some other kind of threat may be used based on what you fear the most.

They **deny their actions** or explain it away. When the occasion comes again when you cross them, they will use abusive actions again. Unless they repent to God and accept their deliverance, they are dangerous. The abuser is **operating in learned behavior**. Either the abuser saw abuse or was abused themselves in the past. They may even deny they were abused growing up. They must come face to face with the issue. They may dodge the pain and continue to cover it up. When they excuse the person who abused them as a child, this puts them in a place of denial and causes grief and perpetuates the same behavior in them. The thing they hate they become. This can be overcome by confessing to God, *"I was abused in my childhood and I do not want to be an abuser. Help me Holy Spirit and forgive me for walking in any of these tendencies. I ask for your divine deliverance."*

## A FAMILIAR SPIRIT

Sometimes the threat from their abuser holds them in bondage even after the abuser has died. This is **a familiar spirit** in action and we have power over it through God's Word. A familiar spirit uses the traits of that person in the past with whom you were familiar. They can cause you to feel the abuser will hear if you tell it. The abuser is not even there, but the fear of them hearing the truth makes you feel their power over you. No one has to be an abuser. They can break the cycle anytime. God will help anyone through a spirit of forgiveness to be free from the fear of the voices that torment.

*Luke 10:19*
*"Behold I give you power to tread on serpents and*

*scorpions, and over all the power of the enemy, and
nothing shall by any means hurt you."*

**Covering up for them will affect your personality.** The abuser loves and hates simultaneously. Their emotions can change immediately. Some abusers control through their silence. Abusive behavior can be a trait of either a man or a woman. You can stay strong if you develop a close relationship with the Holy Spirit and confess His Word over the situation.

**Discipline may be difficult for an abuser.** Either they discipline their children too much or not at all. They hate what happened to them as a child so badly that they cannot even help their children mature through their discipline. This may cause their children to know no boundaries and be aggressive in their behavior toward other people. In my own family we have had to deal with this. Due to abuse, there were no boundaries with each other. We did not realize it, but we crossed lines in each other's lives. This caused conflict in relationships with one another. Learning to set boundaries when there have been none is not easy, but with the help of the Holy Spirit it can be done.

There was a terrible incident in the news several years ago. A man from Northern California, who had been in church with his family on Sunday morning, went home and killed six family members. Their pastor was shocked and had thought all was well in their home. Unfortunately, these kind of things happen. We need to pray *Psalms 91* over our homes often as a means of protection.

*Psalms 91:1-16*

*1 He that dwelleth in the secret place of the most High shall abide under the shadow of the Almighty.*

*2 I will say of the Lord, He is my refuge and my fortress: my God; in him will I trust.*

*3 Surely he shall deliver thee from the snare of the fowler, and from the noisome pestilence.*

*4 He shall cover thee with his feathers, and under his wings shalt thou trust: his truth shall be thy shield and buckler.*

*5 Thou shalt not be afraid for the terror by night; nor for the arrow that flieth by day;*

*6 Nor for the pestilence that walketh in darkness; nor for the destruction that wasteth at noon day.*

*7 A thousand shall fall at thy side, and ten thousand at thy right hand; but it shall not come nigh thee.*

*8 Only with thine eyes shalt thou behold and see the reward of the wicked.*

*9 Because thou hast made the Lord, which is my refuge, even the most High, thy habitation;*

*10 There shall no evil befall thee, neither shall any plague come nigh thy dwelling.*

*11 For he shall give his angels charge over thee, to keep thee in all thy ways.*

*12 They shall bear thee up in their hands, lest thou dash thy foot against a stone.*

*13 Thou shalt tread upon the lion and adder; the young lion and the dragon shalt thou trample under foot.*

*14 Because he hath set his love upon me, therefore*

*will I deliver him: I will set him on high, because he
hath known my name.
15 He shall call upon me, and I will answer him: I
will be with him in trouble; I will deliver him and
honor him.
16 With long life will I satisfy him, and show him my
salvation.*

Living in *Psalms 91* makes all the difference in the world. If
you are in an abusive relationship, you do need to abide under the shadow of the Almighty.

We have covered several kinds of abuse. Each one of us needs
to look at ourselves to see if we are an abuser. You might be
thinking I am not an abuser and I would never abuse anything
or anyone. Here are some questions you might ask yourself:

- Do we abuse things that God has blessed us with?
- Do we speak things continually which hurt those we
  love?
- Do we get angry immediately and blame others for
  mistakes?
- Do we threaten others and ask them not to tell about
  abuse?
- Do we need to control others and use manipulation to
  get our way?

***All kinds of abuse emotionally affect
those that we live and work with.***

## OUR SOCIETY IS ADDICTED TO ABUSIVE BEHAVIOR

Do you ever wonder why there are so many people addicted to various kinds of abusive behavior in our society? Many people are hiding from things which hurt them in the past and are trying to keep from facing the pain. The addictive behavior only delays their deliverance and makes it worse. They run to things for solace rather than face the issue. This is the pattern of abuse in many people's lives.

I am so glad that I never had to deal with a problem like Tamar did. The whole thing is sickening. I can only imagine how the things she dealt with must have hurt her. Many of you may have had to deal with incest. I have five brothers and not anytime in my life have I ever felt uneasy with them. That is the way it should be, but that is not always the way it is. Through the **delivering power of God**, we can see some normalcy return to people's lives.

**Notes:** _____

_____

_____

_____

_____

_____

_____

_____

**Notes:** _____

_____
_____
_____
_____
_____
_____
_____
_____
_____
_____
_____
_____
_____
_____
_____
_____
_____
_____
_____
_____
_____
_____
_____
_____
_____
_____
_____
_____
_____

# CHAPTER 10
## Ignoring Signals Before Marriage

■ ■ ■ ■ ■ ■ ■ ■ ■ ■

**Marrying the wrong person** is another thing that can make a person a victim. God gives us **warning signals** before we marry someone who is abusive. Through our own needs we can miss the things God would show us or speak to our hearts.

I found this article in the paper. The heading says, **"Wife regrets ignoring signs that warned of bad marriage."** It related this story:

Two weeks ago, my husband let it slip that he wants a divorce. Since we were married, his personality has changed completely. He is not the man I married. I would like to pass along some tips for anyone considering marriage, and share some of the bright-red flags I chose to ignore.

▶ **1.** If your parents or siblings have doubts about him, pay attention. Listen and check it out.

▶ **2.** If your intended has nothing good to say about his ex-wife, beware.   Divorce is rarely only one person's fault.

▶ **3.** If his children have nothing to do with him, do not believe him if he says his ex-wife brainwashed them against him.  My stepchildren have told me it was because they hated him, and they have good reasons.

▶ **4.** Look closely at his credit and job history.  They are sure predictors of what your life will be like.

▶ **5.** If he's over 30 and has no money, do not let him move in with you, and don't marry him until he's financially solvent.

▶ **6.** Be sure in your heart that you can live with him AS IS.  You cannot change another person.

▶ **7.** Beware if he has no friends.  It is not true they all chose to side with his ex.

▶ **8.** If your friends dislike him, pay attention.  This is also true if he hates your friends.

▶ **9.** If he has more than one DUI and still drinks, run!

▶ **10.** If he is one personality at work or with others, and another person alone with you, run!

▶ **11.** If he has nothing to do with his parents, investigate why.  Don't take his word for it.

▶ **12.** If he's an expert at everything and brags a lot, understand that he will turn off a lot of people, eventually maybe even you.

▶ **13.** If he has sexual problems, go with him to a doctor before you marry him.  Believe me his problem will become your problem later.

▶ **14.** If he is emotionally or verbally abusive, it will only get worse.  Yelling, name-calling and sullen anger are classic signs of an abuser.

▶ **15.** If he is never wrong and never apologizes, everything will be "your fault" forever.  And after years, you may even start to accept all the blame.

▶ **16.** If he does something wrong and says, "That wouldn't have happened **if you hadn't** (...... ) that's another sign of an abuser.

▶ **17.** And if he's mean to children, pets or animals, recognize that he's pathological and the next victim could be you.

This lady is now 100 percent disabled and in danger of losing everything.  She was **taken in** by someone who came to regard her as a disposable item.  I only hope her letter will save someone else from the heartbreak she experienced.

This is a typical example of a person who was **victimized in marriage** as we can see clearly from her letter.  She did not listen to the cautions of others.  So many times this is the case.  We need to talk to the Lord about our relationships and listen to his voice concerning what he tells us to do.  There are persons who would not be taken in, if they would listen to the Holy Spirit.  When we know the Lord, we have divine discernment to help us in every situation of life.

## SPEAKING THE TRUTH IN LOVE

*Ephesians 4:14-15 AMPC*
*14 So then, we may no longer be children, tossed [like ships] to and fro between chance gusts [the prey of] the cunning and cleverness of unscrupulous men, [gamblers engaged] in every shifting form of trickery in inventing errors to mislead.*

*15 But speaking the truth in love, may <u>grow up</u> into him in all things, which is the head, even Christ.*

Truth in this Scripture means to be true in doctrine and profession. God's Word does not make room for hatefulness toward others. It does make room for correction in love. To be true to the profession and calling is to help people **mature** by using the Word of God to bring correction and instruction.

In ministry, we should know those who labor among us. It is not uncommon anymore that those who work with children must fill out a police report. Some people balk at that, and it causes me to wonder why.

> *Galatians 1:7 AMP*
> *. . . there are obviously some who are troubling and disturbing you [with a different kind of teaching which they offer as a gospel] and want to pervert and distort <u>the Gospel of Christ</u> (the Messiah) [into something which it absolutely is not].*

If the Gospel of Christ is being taught with purpose and freedom, then there is no perverting of the Gospel. The **<u>misuse of spiritual authority</u>** is serious business with God. We need to be true to the doctrine of Christ and true to the profession for which he has called us.

**Notes:** _____

_____

_____

_____

_____

_____

_____

_____

_____

_____

_____

_____

_____

_____

_____

_____

_____

_____

_____

_____

_____

_____

_____

_____

_____

_____

_____

_____

_____

_____

**Notes:** _____

_____
_____
_____
_____
_____
_____
_____
_____
_____
_____
_____
_____
_____
_____
_____
_____
_____
_____
_____
_____
_____
_____
_____
_____
_____
_____
_____
_____
_____

# CHAPTER 11
## Enabling and Rescuing

■ ■ ■ ■ ■ ■ ■ ■ ■ ■ ■

### ENABLING

The subject of abuse leads us to the topic of enabling. **The word enable means to give legal power, capacity or sanction to. It also means to supply with the means, knowledge, and the chance to be or do something.** *Webster's New Collegiate Dictionary*

Enabling is allowing someone to continue to have power over you in a detrimental sense. I have seen people who are major enablers in the wrong sense, which means they **give people power** to hinder others from spiritual growth by sanctioning their behavior. Those called into the ministry have a mercy gift. God uses that gift to help people who are in despair. When this gift gets twisted or perverted by people, it affects the whole congregation. In the past I would try to put people forward in ministry because they said they were called to be in ministry, but quite a few were using the ministry to hide their misbehavior. The Lord helped me to **discern** between those who wanted to obey God and those who were using the position in ministry to hide their misbehavior. We have lots of *ministry want-a-bes*. To want to be a minister is noble, but not to want to pay the price for the God-Called ministry goes no place. I have dealt with some uncomfortable things in order not to enable someone in the ministry to hurt others. Sometimes people see what they think is a glamorous position in ministry and want to be there. They do not see how the requirements of living a holy life can have a lasting effect on their ministry. There is a price to be paid by those who are going to minister to others. Willingness to pay that price is what God is looking for.

We have the power to be **a good enabler** through Christ Jesus. God has called us to help others. When we offer our lives to Christ, He gives so much back to us in exchange. We then share His goodness with others.

## FORGIVENESS

*1 Timothy 1:12-13 (KJV)*
*12 "And I thank Christ Jesus our Lord, who hath enabled me, for that he counted me faithful, putting me into the ministry.*
*13 "Who was before a blasphemer, and a persecutor, and injurious: but I obtained mercy, because I did it ignorantly in unbelief."*

Paul was speaking about his life before he knew Christ. Only

God could forgive his sin. Paul was the one who had Stephen killed.

> *Acts 7:54-60*
> *54 When they heard these things, they were cut to the heart, and they gnashed on him with their teeth.*
> *55 But he, being full of the Holy Ghost, looked up steadfastly into heaven, and saw the glory of God, and Jesus standing on the right hand of God.*
> *56 And said, Behold, I see the heavens opened, and the Son of man standing on the right hand of God.*
> *57 Then they cried out with a loud voice, and stopped their ears, and ran upon him with one accord,*
> *58 and cast him out of the city, and stoned him: and the witnesses laid down their clothes at a young man's feet, whose name was Saul.*
> *59 And they stoned Stephen, calling upon God, and saying, Lord Jesus, receive my spirit.*
> *60 And he kneeled down, and cried with a loud voice, Lord, lay not this sin to their charge. And when he had said this, he fell asleep.*

Thank God for Jesus and the price that he paid for **<u>forgiveness</u>**. Saul enabled others to stone Stephen. After Christ he enabled people to do good things for God. He was totally changed by the encounter he had with the Lord on the road to Damascus. We do not see Paul continuing this horrible behavior once he had received Christ. He was **forgiven** and set free to minister to others.

All of us have been forgiven of things that we wish we had never done.

> *Romans 3:23* says,
> *All of us have sinned and fallen short of the glory of God.*

When I speak of forgiveness and unforgiveness, I want to make it clear, I am not asking you to hold someone's sin against them. Sometimes people are not sorry for their sin; just sorry they got caught. <u>There is a big difference.</u> Saul was sorry for what he did to the believers. God is the one who caught him, shook him up, and blinded him for three days. God sent him to Ananias who prayed for him and God restored his sight. Paul was totally forgiven by God, but it took time for restoration. During this proving period Paul was lifted up and made strong in the area he had previously failed.

The standard for forgiveness is shown through Paul.

> *2 Timothy 4:14-15*
> *14 "Alexander the coppersmith did me great wrongs. The Lord will pay him back for his actions.*
> *15 "Beware of him yourself, for he opposed and resist-ed our message very strongly and exceedingly."*

Was Paul in unforgiveness because he warned others about what Alexander the coppersmith did? Not really. He told them that he was strongly opposing the message of the gospel and was trying to do the church harm. Paul was not go-

ing to continue to **enable him** to do that. He was being protective of the church. Paul knew about this kind of thing.
He had done harm to the Church himself.

Paul was in training to walk the Christian walk. For fourteen
years the Holy Spirit taught him as we see referenced below.

> *2 Corinthians 12:2-3 KJV*
> *2 "I knew a man in Christ above fourteen years ago,*
> *(whether in the body, I cannot tell; or whether out of*
> *the body, I cannot tell: God knoweth;) such an one*
> *caught up to the third heaven.*
> *3 "And I knew such a man, (whether in the body, or*
> *out of the body, I cannot tell: God knoweth;)"*

Sometimes we hear about actors or actresses, ball players
etc. getting born-again. They have been in the world, but
now they have changed to serve Christ. Some of them begin
well, but do not last. They were not able to get the proper
training and support and therefore their foundation is not
strong. There are others who take the time to build a solid
foundation and become a great influence for Christ. George
Foreman was a boxer. He is now a pastor in Los Angeles who
helps youth to get a good start in life. It is better to be established in God's Word and stay strong to help others than to
give a testimony that is tried. Many fall due to not having a
good foundation spiritually.

If you know of a "**con**" who has entered the church and is
taking advantage of people, you should allow your leaders to

have this knowledge to help warn others concerning them. If you did not warn others, you would be **enabling** them to do harm. I feel the enemy has tried to rob the Church of some of its power by blinding us in this area. One of the safest ways to guard your heart is to ask yourself, *"Do I want revenge on that person, or can I bless them without reservation?"*

So many of us say, *"How can I ask God to bless them?"* The Word tells us to bless them ourselves with the words of our mouth.

> *Matthew 10:12-13*
> *12 "And when you come into an house, salute it.*
> *13 "And if the house be worthy let your peace come upon it: but if it be not worthy, let your peace return to you."*

## HOW TO SPOT A CON

Recently I was reading an article in a magazine, **Ministries Today,** entitled *'How to Spot a Holy Con'.* The little insert says, *"They speak in tongues, prophesy, and tell stories of missionary exploits. Is their next victim your church?"* The whole article was about one woman who went about deceiving men, women, pastors or whoever would believe her. One man who had just gone through a divorce, met her and she appeared to be the perfect **Proverbs 31 Woman**. This man was enchanted by her personality. She let it be known she was looking for a Boaz. Soon this man was offering her money. He gave her access to his credit cards <u>early on in the relationship</u>. He said, *"I thought God was having mercy* *on me and bringing me somebody to fulfill my destiny."* He asked her to marry him. He lavished her with everything she wanted totaling around $60,000. On their wedding night she became hostile and indifferent which lasted for months. His unwillingness to go get help, cost him dearly. When they married he had no debt, but he would eventually lose it all. Why didn't he insist on a visit with the pastor for counseling? He felt like a prisoner in his own home trapped there with a critical, physiologically abusive mate who, just a few months earlier, was so much the answer to all of his prayers. By the end of the year, she had vanished after charging over $100,000 on credit cards. He had to sell his house to pay off all the debts. This same woman later showed up in another place and tried a similar thing on another divorced man.

His pastor warned other pastors to keep a more careful watch on their congregations. In any congregation there will likely be a few persons who are more vulnerable due to their situations and can become targets for these "cons." A pastor should be cautious when asked to perform a hasty wedding between a wealthy parishioner and a future spouse who is unknown.

How are these people going to treat this situation? They certainly need to be able to warn others about this person. Forgive them for your own benefit, but you are not required to ever have a relationship with them.

You do not necessarily have to ask God to bless them. If they are not deserving of the blessing, then God will cause it to come back to you.

*Luke 10:5-6*
*5 And into whatsoever house ye enter, first say, Peace be to this house.*
*6 And if the son of peace be there, your peace shall rest upon it: if not, it shall turn to you again.*

As we have seen these things concerning **enabling** in both good and bad examples, we can recognize where we may have been trapped. The Holy Spirit taught me much about these things during times of condemnation. I thought I was in **unforgiveness** when I felt someone needed to be proven. When I began to see these things, insincere people did not come around me as often as they used to. As I have progressed in the Lord's work, I always ask God for a discerning heart to love the people through Him.

## USERS OR GIVERS

As we look at this topic, ask yourself, *"Am I a user or a giver?"* The nature of Christ is to be a giver. **Give** has various meanings. *One is to make a present of. It means to deliver in exchange or recompense. To be a source of good or bad.*

**A <u>user</u> is someone who exploits for one's own advantage or gain. An example is using someone else to get ahead and leaving them without any support.**

Giving and using can both be good and bad. It has to do with the purpose for which we are doing something. To exploit others for our own gain is not good. *If we are selfish and exploit others, then we are a user in the negative sense.* As we learn to use things properly, we will bless people and not misuse them. Keep **giving and using** in the positive sense.

A good example of misuse and abuse is the building God gave to our ministry in Oklahoma. The place had been abused and was being used by others to promote the programs of the enemy. We went in and started using it for God's glory. We cleaned, decorated, and restored it. God used the building to house missionaries. We used something that God put into our hands for His Glory!

## AM I A RESCUER?

*The word rescue means to save, as from imprisonment or danger. 2. To deliver from legal custody by force.*

**Rescue** is a good word. The song, *My Redeemer Lives*, has words in it that say, *I know He rescued my soul, His blood has covered my sin, I believe, I believe.* Actually Christ has not covered our sins but destroyed them.

In another sense of rescue, we may find ourselves in a situation where people do not want to be rescued and they pull us down with them. I certainly would not try to save someone who is drowning if I did not know how to swim. My knowledge would be limited, unless I had taken a course in life guarding.

In an article, I read about a person who had a great heart.

He loved the Lord and loved people.  He married a woman who had a child. She needed help, and he thought that he could help her.  He made bad decisions without the help of the Lord.  He kept bailing this lady out of financial situations and even helped her start her own business.  This all sounds great and noble, but he got into so much financial trouble that he could not get out.  <u>She left the marriage</u> and he was overloaded with her unpaid bills. He also quit going to church.  When we put our life in jeopardy ***to rescue others*** we are like the person who is trying to be a lifeguard and does not know how to swim.  **Both lives are in danger of being destroyed.**

When we are in the ministry, we do **rescue people**. Many times I have seen ministers get into trouble because they wanted to help people without setting boundaries in their own home. Sometimes they bring people into their home who cause confusion and unrest.  When that needy person has used them for a while, they go find someone else to use.  If you choose to rescue someone, be sure you set boundaries up front both in the family schedule and finances. If there is **weakness in the authority** of the home, you leave an open door for problems to arise. Ministers need to be strong in the Lord.

If we are **counseling** someone, it is best if they live elsewhere. If they live with you, they become too close and may not listen anymore.  Your human faults can become a weapon against you.  **Enabling and rescuing** are so similar.  We do not marry someone to rescue them.  We can get back into the victim mentality if we do. T.D. Jakes says, *"Get yourself a job, get your-*

*self some good insurance, get out of debt and let God send to you someone who blesses your life."* Too many people get into trouble because they just need someone to rescue. Rescuing the other person may jeopardize your identity and self worth.

Have you ever been rescued? _____

_____

_____

_____

_____

_____

Have you rescued someone else? _____

_____

_____

_____

_____

_____

_____

## Notes: _____

_____

_____

_____

_____

_____

_____

_____

**Notes:** _____

_____

_____

_____

_____

_____

_____

_____

_____

_____

_____

_____

_____

_____

_____

_____

_____

_____

_____

_____

_____

_____

_____

_____

_____

_____

_____

_____

# CHAPTER 12
## Protecting the Widow

■ ■ ■ ■ ■ ■ ■ ■ ■ ■ ■ ■

We can depend on God who is faithful and trustworthy. He is our source and he is our Rescuer. I have tested this as a widow. Widows can become victims so quickly if they do not stay focused on the Lord. *Isaiah 54:5-6* lets us know that Jesus is our husband and redeemer. *I Timothy 5:3-5* speaks of how a widow is to behave. She is to be a consecrated person unto the Lord. If she is dedicated to the Lord then she will be who she is supposed to be in Christ, and her life will be blessed.

Many times in the Word of God instructions are given for the widow.

*1 Timothy 5:3-5 Honor widows that are widows indeed...* this is the widow who has no one to help her. She may not have had children or her children may have deserted her. They could just be insensitive to her needs. It may be someone whose husband is still alive but does nothing to bless her life. There is a saying, "grass widow" meaning one who is alone even though she is married. We usually think of it as a woman whose husband has died.

*Isaiah 54:4-5*
*4 Fear not; for thou shalt not be ashamed: neither be thou confounded; for thou shalt not be put to shame: for thou shalt forget the shame of thy youth, and shalt not remember the reproach of thy widowhood any more.*
*5 For thy Maker is thine husband; the Lord of hosts is his name: and thy Redeemer the Holy One of Israel: The God of the whole earth shall he be called.*

*James 1:27*
*Pure religion and undefiled before God and the Father is this, To visit the fatherless and widows in their affliction, and to keep himself unspotted from the world.*

*Exodus 22:22-23*
*22 Ye shall not afflict any widow or fatherless child.*
*23 If thou afflict them in any wise, and they cry out to me, I will surely hear their cry.*

God has spoken specific words concerning the care of the widows and the fatherless. He promises the widow He is her husband. The Amplified Bible speaks of the consecrated widow as having a border around her.

*Proverbs 15:25 AMP*
*The Lord tears down the house of the proud, but He makes secure the boundaries of the [consecrated] widow.*

This verse assures the consecrated widow of secure boundaries. **Consecrate** means *to devote entirely or dedicate.* A widow who is dedicated to the Lord is the one who has these rights with God. The King James Version says He establishes the boundary of the widow.

In Strong's 5324 the word **establish** means *station, appointed, deputy, erect, establish. It means to lay, officer, pillar, present, rear up, set (over, up) settle, sharpen, stablish, (make to) stand.*

In the dictionary **establish** means *to make stable; make firm; settle.*

It seems this verse is saying God takes special care to place guards around the widow for protection.

I have seen my whole mindset change because of the previously mentioned scriptures. **Sometimes a widow feels abandoned.** She may not feel right with married people or realize her children do not understand her present needs now that she is a widow. Some widows adapt more quickly than others. Getting the Word of God inside your heart as a new widow will make you stronger. If we draw from God's provision during these times of life, we will trust His ability to help us.

## DEALING WITH ABANDONMENT ISSUES

The first year maybe you have decided to do something different with your family and you don't notice it was bad as you thought it would be.  Our family chose to go to Disney Land together that first year.  The next two years I did something on my own along with a friend and celebrated Christmas with the family at a different time.  One year I was invited to my daughter, Mary Charlene's in-laws' beautiful home.  Everyone was kind but I began to cry.  I felt ashamed to be crying but I could not seem to hold it back.  Thoughts began to go through my mind of how the support of me with the ministry had not seemed to be there.  I thought of how friends brought funds to us while he was alive, but after he was gone, after a couple years, it was not the same.  This was a good lesson for me to learn to overcome this despairing feeling.  I felt neglected and abandoned.  I had never had this feeling before and frankly, afterwards I felt disappointed in myself.  I questioned why the funds had not come like they used to.  Today I would never do such a thing.  My faith has been built up to keep my eyes on the Lord and not blame people for any lack.

I got alone with God and asked Him what in the world happened to me? He spoke so gently to me, *"You are dealing with an abandonment issue."* If you are like me, if you know what you are dealing with you can overcome it quicker.  As I have shared my heart with you about this issue, my testimony of overcoming is in the next paragraph.  I have learned to focus on Jesus as my divine supplier.

When my husband passed away in 1998, I had to make big decisions. God walked me through every step I had to take. Sometimes things were very tight financially, but God always brought me through. *Widows can make good decisions with*

***God's help each day.*** We can also educate ourselves in areas where we may need help. In certain weak areas, the Lord would send others who were developed in that particular area to help me. I learned to completely **trust in the Lord at all times.**

The Scriptures tell us exactly what our responsibility is toward widows and orphans. I mentioned it in the above Scriptures but I want to point it out again.

> *James 1:27 KJV*
> *Pure religion and undefiled before God and the Father is this, to visit the fatherless and widows in their affliction, and to keep himself unspotted from the world.*

Godly people are around me who live this Scripture from *James 1:27.* Recently God opened the door for me to get a new house. The house didn't come with a refrigerator, a washer/dryer, blinds etc. In my heart, I knew God would provide but I had no clue of how it would happen. God spoke to a friend, she contacted a ministry I am involved in. She asked if she could let people know about my new home and the needs I had. When she spoke to them about it, they quoted the above Scripture *James 1:27.* They became doers of the Word of God. Within a week or so, God had used my friend and partners who found out about my needs and all the items I needed were met.

As soon as I had the keys in my hands, my friend said, *"We are going shopping."* She announced to me, we are purchasing a new refrigerator, washer and dryer and blinds. I was stunned. She told me the money needed for these items had been raised. WOW! What a blessing! Today I have lived there for a couple years and so much has been done to make this house my home. I encourage every widow to watch God work in your behalf. Don't waste a minute in despair.

Other Scriptures showing God's heart toward the widow are...
*Deuteronomy 24:17*
*Thou shalt not pervert the judgment of the stranger, [nor] of the fatherless; nor take a widow's raiment to pledge:*

*Deuteronomy 14:28-29 AMPC*
*28 At the end of three years thou shalt bring forth all the tithe of thine increase the same year, and shalt lay [it] up within thy gates:*
*29 And the Levite, (because he hath no part nor inheritance with thee,) and the stranger, and the fatherless, and the widow, which [are] within thy gates, shall come, and shall eat and be satisfied; that the LORD thy God may bless thee in all the work of thine hand which thou doest.*

I admonish the body of Christ, be sensitive to the needs of the widow.

**Notes:** _____
_____
_____
_____
_____

# CHAPTER 13
## Thinking Victoriously

■ ■ ■ ■ ■ ■ ■ ■ ■ ■ ■ ■ ■

We need to allow God's Word to heal us of **victim thinking**. If you will read and focus on these verses below, you will begin to think victoriously!

*Psalms 4:6-7 AMPC*
*6 Many say, Oh, that we might see good! Lift up the light of Your countenance upon us, O Lord,*
*7 Thou hast put gladness in my heart, more than in the time that their corn and their wine increased.*

*Psalms 13:5-6 AMPC*
*5 But I have trusted, leaned on, and been confident in Your mercy and loving-kindness. My heart shall rejoice and be in high spirits in Your salvation.*
*6 I will sing unto the Lord, because he has dealt bountifully with me.*

*Psalms 15:1-5 AMP*
*1 Lord, who shall dwell [temporarily] in your taber-*

nacle? Who shall live [permanently] on your holy hill?

2 He who walks and lives uprightly and blamelessly, who works rightness and justice and speaks and thinks the truth in his heart,

3 He who does not slander with his tongue, nor does evil to his friend, nor takes up a reproach against his neighbor;

4 In whose eyes a vile person is despised, but he who honors those who fear the Lord (who revere and worship Him); who swears to his own hurt and does not change.

5 [He who] does not put out his money for interest [to one of his own people] and who will not take a bribe against the innocent. He who does these things shall never be moved.

Proverbs 4:20-23

20 My son, attend to my words; incline thine ear unto my sayings,

21 Let them not depart from thine eye; keep them in the midst of thine heart.

22 For they are life unto those that find them, and health to all their flesh.

23 Keep thy heart with all diligence; for out of it are the issues of life.

Luke 6:45

A good man out of the good treasure of his heart bringeth forth that which is good; and an evil man out of the evil treasure of his heart bringeth forth that which is evil; for out of the abundance of the heart the mouth speaketh.

*Ephesians 6:6*
*Not with eye service, as men pleasers; but as the servants of Christ, doing the will of God from the heart.*

From all these Scriptures we can see **God wants us to have confidence in Him.** He can deliver us from anything if we allow Him. He tells us to fill ourselves with Him and His Word. If we do this, we will be healed in every area of our life.

## RENEWING OUR MIND

*Ephesians 4:23*
*Be renewed in the spirit of your mind.*

The word **renewed** in this Scripture means *to renovate.* The word **renew** from the dictionary means *to make new or as if new again.* The word **spirit** in this Scripture means *your rational soul.* The word **mind** means *intellect. It means in thought, feelings, will, or in your understanding.*

If we renovate something, we make it like new. Old houses get renovated and remodeled to look different. Outwardly they may have the same address, but they have been changed. It is the same with us. Others realize something about us is different.

To be **renewed** takes action on our part. Renewal is a process of something that we do in our soul. The word **mind** means *our intellect.* We have charge of the way we think. Our mind, will, and emotions have to be **renovated** by the power of God through the Word.  If we keep the Word of God before us, we will get our minds renewed.  Some of the ways to put the Word of God in our minds is through listening to **worship music, Bible teaching, and sermons.** Sometimes a particular Scripture or teaching point will stand out for us. *Ephesians 3:23* says for us to *be renewed in the spirit of your mind.*

We cannot allow circumstances to cause us to say, *"I am sick!"* Our renewed minds think, *"I am healed!"* and according to *Isaiah 53:5 . . . with His stripes we are healed.* We do not deny we are ill, but deny it's power over us. That is how we retrain our thinking to agree with God's Word. You might say, *"I am broke!"* but God's Word says *He supplies all my need according to His riches in glory by Christ Jesus. (Philippians 4:19)*  He will give you favor for a job or career as you confess, *I am willing and obedient, I shall eat of the good of the land.  (Isaiah1:19)*

That is how we fill our minds.  <u>**We must speak it out of our mouths.**</u>  The devil has blinded many people who say nothing and get nothing.  <u>**We must speak the Word.**</u>  It is not good enough to just think it.

> *Mark 11:23*
> *Say to the mountain be thou removed and cast into the sea; and shall not doubt in his heart, but shall believe those things which he saith, shall come to pass; he shall have whatsoever he saith.*

## BE A DOER OF THE WORD

*James 1:22* instructs us to *be doers of the Word, and not hearers only, deceiving your own selves.*

The devil does not even have to come up with something to deceive us with. If we are not putting our mouth in line with the Word of God, we will deceive our own selves.

> *James 1:2*
> *My brethren, count it all joy when ye fall into divers temptations.*

If it says to count it all joy, then I must begin to laugh, leap, shout or whatever it takes to get into joy. That is doing the Word.

We have dealt with some pretty heavy subjects during this teaching.

**Victim mentality can be overcome** by knowing what the Word says about being victorious. <u>**We can choose to have a victor's mentality**</u> by applying victorious thinking. *Abuse is misuse of any person or thing.* By not using the Word of God we are abusing it. We are blessed with prosperity in our lives when we choose to speak God's Word.

We overcome all these things by His anointing using God's Word. We will walk in victory and be successful as we move on toward wholeness in our mind, will, and emotions.

**Notes:** _____

_____
_____
_____
_____
_____
_____
_____
_____
_____
_____
_____
_____
_____
_____
_____
_____
_____
_____
_____
_____
_____
_____
_____
_____
_____
_____
_____

# CHAPTER 14
## Reflecting

■ ■ ■ ■ ■ ■ ■ ■ ■ ■ ■ ■ ■ ■ ■

There is not one person who reads this book who has not been victimized in some way. I hope this book has helped you to recognize satan's lies. He always deals in fear and tries to keep us in bondage through it. Just because you are a Christian does not keep you from being touched in some area. The Word of God can reach into the depths of your heart and heal you. I admonish you to listen to your spirit as to hear God before you become a victim. If you have the scratchy feeling or a halt in pit of your stomach, listen and go no further. That is a check in your spirit from God. It will spare you of a lot of difficulty.

### Reflection

Take a few minutes to get quiet in the presence of the Lord. Let Him reach down into your soul and **heal the area of most concern to you.** The Holy Spirit knows your deepest need and will minister peace to your heart. Write some notes to help you remember how to keep your peace.

**Notes:** _____

_____
_____
_____
_____
_____
_____
_____
_____
_____
_____
_____
_____
_____
_____
_____
_____
_____
_____
_____
_____
_____
_____
_____
_____
_____
_____

## ● RECOMMENDED READING ●

*I recommend the following books as the Lord led me to them during a time of tragedy.*

- **Beauty for Ashes** and **Battlefield of the Mind** *by Joyce Meyer*

- **Deadly Emotions** *by Dr. Don Colbert*

- **Love is a Choice** *by Minirth/Meier/Hemfelt*

- **Don't Let the Jerks Get the Best of You** *by Meier*

- **An Affair of the Mind** *by Laurie Hall*

## ● SOCIAL MEDIA ●

**WIDOWS WITH PURPOSE** is a group page on Facebook devoted to ministering to those whose loved ones have moved on to Heaven. You are invited to join to receive articles written daily to uplift and encourage the widow, widower or those who are alone.

**Rachel Jeffries International Ministries** page is also available on Facebook.

## ● CONTACT INFORMATION ●

To order more books, schedule speaking engagements or other correspondence:

*www.rjim.org*
Rachel Jeffries International Ministries
P.O. Box 815
Hollister, Missouri 65673
email: *racheljeffries@msn.com*

Rachel is a songwriter as well as a recording artist.
Her CDs **AMAZING LOVE** A 2 CD PACKAGE AND
**ATMOSPHERE OF PRAYER AND WORSHIP**
are available on ITUNES and SPOTIFY as well
as the ministry website *www.rjim.org*

### ● Other books available ●
*by Rachel V Jeffries*

## CAPTURE A CITY THROUGH PRAISE
*A handbook on intercessory praise.*

This is a teaching of the highest form of prayer in spiritual warfare and how victorious living is so possible through praise.

**PITIFUL OR POWERFUL**
THE CHOICE IS YOURS

Is the first book in a series called,
**THE ROAD TO WHOLENESS.**

*(This book)* **VICTIM TO VICTOR**
is the second book in this series.

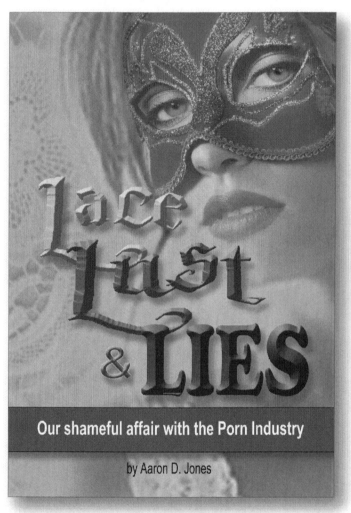

98324867R00072

Made in the USA
Columbia, SC
23 June 2018